Mobilising Capital for Emerging Markets

Doris Köhn
Editor

Mobilising Capital for Emerging Markets

What Can Structured Finance Contribute?

Springer

Editor
Doris Köhn
Senior Vice President Africa
and Middle East
Palmengartenstr. 5
KfW Entwicklungsbank
60325 Frankfurt am Main
Germany
info@kfw-entwicklungsbank.de

ISBN 978-3-642-43100-5 ISBN 978-3-540-92225-4 (eBook)
DOI 10.1007/978-3-540-92225-4
Springer Heidelberg Dordrecht London New York

Cover design: eStudio Calamar S.L.

Cover illustration: www.shutterstock.com

Printed on acid-free paper

Springer is part of Springer Science+Business Media (www.springer.com)

Preface

Is structured finance dead? Many have asked this question after the financial crisis. Or is structured finance "evil" and therefore should it be dead? We at KfW think neither nor. Structured finance is an instrument which can be very useful if well used in an appropriate context. It can also be useful for reaching development objectives. As any instrument, not just in the financial sector, it can also be misused or applied under inappropriate conditions. This was certainly the case in the US subprime housing market and in a few other cases. However financial sectors in emerging markets have proven to be far more resilient in the crisis and we believe there are many examples where structured finance has proven an effective tool to support financial sector development.

The development of financial sectors in emerging markets is a key pillar in KfW's strategy to fight poverty. Over the past two decades we have increased our efforts in this area, especially in microfinance. We consider providing capital and investment opportunities to be an effective tool for developing markets to boost enterprise growth, employment and fight poverty.

In our approach we support our development partners in developing enabling sector policies, legislation, and regulation. This is complemented by building institutions at the regulatory as well as the market intermediary levels. Mobilizing domestic capital through savings and the capital markets in order to facilitate productive investment is at the heart of this approach.

However, emerging markets often require additional efforts to introduce good international practice, modern management skills and long term capital. Recognizing this need we have over the last decade selectively introduced and subsequently increased the use of structured finance, including securitization. Relying on its dedicated emerging market and securitization know-how KfW Group is using structured finance (i) in the securitization of SME and microfinance portfolios, and (ii) in funds with risk subordination to boost private investment.

We work with private and public investment partners based on their reputation as patient and responsible investors and rather avoid investors and investees with a short term orientation. This shared long term view has proven to be useful during the recent global financial crisis, which was partly triggered by inappropriate structured finance.

We are proud to say that more than three years since onset of the crisis our structured finance investments in emerging markets are doing well, although some countries have been hit hard. The patience of investors and reinforced efforts of supporting affected partner institutions played an important part in this success.

Irrespective of this positive experience the crisis has shown the widespread abuse of instruments in the absence of transparency, sound judgment of market participants, and often a lack of prudent oversight. Structured finance in emerging markets therefore requires debate of the lessons learnt from a crisis that originated in the West with the collapse of the sub-prime housing market in the US.

This book reflects feed-back that we seek from development and market partners and experts to undertake a reality check and outlook for future operations. Structured finance in developing countries was the topic of KfW's financial sector symposium in November 2007, when the crisis was about to unfold. The authors of the chapters to take into account the experience of the crisis.

In light of the crisis Michael Klein sets the stage with his overview discussing structured finance as an ambiguous financial tool. This is followed by the various authors' inquiry under which conditions structured finance is suitable for emerging markets The second part of the book looks at the applications of structured finance in support of SME and microfinance. This includes activities as diverse as mitigation and adaptation to climate change, infrastructure development, remittances, rural livelihood, and Shari'ah-compliant Islamic finance.

The diverse application of structured finance underscores its usefulness as a tool for mobilizing capital for development and the need to carefully assess the motivations and backgrounds of investment partners and the soundness of investments. Short-sighted return motivation and overly complex structures are certainly warning signs. Structured finance and securitization will remain an important instrument for development finance.

I would like to thank the German Government and FMO of the Netherland for sponsoring the International Symposium, the authors for their efforts in preparing and revising the papers and not least my colleagues who made this publication possible especially Cerstin Sander, Rainer Hartel and Giuseppe Violante, for editing and overseeing the production of this book.

April 2011

Doris Köhn
KfW Entwicklungsbank
Senior Vice President Private and Financial Sector
and Africa and Middle East Regions

Table of Contents

CHAPTER 1

Securitization: Wonder Drug or Financial Alchemy?

Michael Klein[*]

The Question: What to Make of Securitization?

The global financial crisis of recent years erupted when securitization failed on a large scale. US subprime mortgage-backed securities became the worst performing asset class in the world (IMF, 2010). Today, criticism of securitization abounds. Reform proposals range from wide-ranging improvements of incentives and disclosure rules to calls for the complete abolition of "the devil's derivatives".[1]

It was not always so. Just before the crisis, securitization was hailed as the answer to all sorts of financing problems. Development banks were admonished to be more risk-seeking and support "these diversified structures [that] have proven track records largely in developed markets but [that] also hold promise for enabling developing country borrowers' access to local and international capital markets" (World Economic Forum, 2006).

As the fog of the crisis lifts, a re-appraisal of securitization is underway with significant implications for development finance. This essay sets out the issues and tentative lessons.

What Is Securitization?

Take mortgage-securitization. Banks or other mortgage originators create a mortgage, which funds some type of real estate, say a house. Instead of holding on to the mortgage and keeping it on their books the originators pass the mortgage to a

---

* Professor Frankfurt School of Finance and Management and Senior Visiting Professor at Johns Hopkins University.

1 As an example consider this blogpost on September 11, 2009 on demonderivatives. blogspot.com: "The 'Lords of the Air and the Underworld' (greedy, demonic psychopaths of wealth and power) aren't going to change this system of funny money and wallstreet casino because it makes a lot of money for the über rich, and besides, if they go broke, they'll just get another Trouble Asset Relief Program (TARP) or TRAP package from the government. Isn't that how it works?"

special purpose vehicle, typically a trust of some type. The trust assembles or "pools" mortgages, typically several thousands. It then sells securities, which are backed by the cash flow from the pool of mortgages. The revenue from the sale of securities pays off any original financier. Now the buyers of securities own pieces of a mix of mortgages – a mortgage-backed security (MBS).

Typically, mortgage-backed securities are sold in "tranches". When several thousand mortgages are pooled, one can statistically estimate that a large percentage of the cash flow will be available no matter what, because most mortgage holders will pay what they have to. One can then create and sell a high-quality or "senior" tranche of securities with almost no default risk, which is served first from the cash flow received by the special purpose vehicle. If cash flow is left-over, it will service a second, lower quality tranche, for which repayment risk is higher. This would be a "mezzanine" tranche. A third "junior" tranche can then be created, which gets serviced from all the cash flow that remains when the more senior tranches have been serviced. Generally, one can subdivide tranches further into securities with different levels of default risk.

The same financing approach can be applied to other forms of assets, for example, credit cards or car loans. In principle, all sorts of assets that generate cash flow can be pooled and then securitized. For example, in 1997, in the first securitization of intellectual property the current and future revenues from 25 albums (287 songs) recorded by David Bowie prior to 1990 were securitized.

Complexity in mortgage-based securities increased as issuers created securities backed by a portfolio of MBS – so called Collateralized Debt Obligations (CDOs)

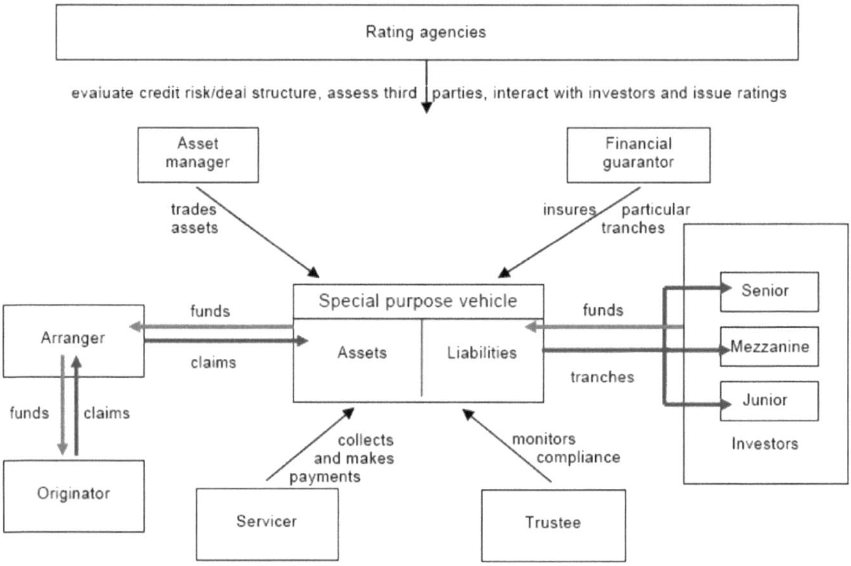

Fig. 1. Securitisation markets: key participants and their roles

Source: Bank for International Settlement (2009)

with typically some 150 MBS in a CDO pool. In turn CDOs were pooled and against such pools "CDOs-squared" were sold with normally around 125 CDOs in the pool.

Rating agencies rate the default risk of securities. The best senior tranches may be rated "AAA", the worst tranches would have "junk bond" status. To improve the quality (and rating) of a tranche, a financial guarantor may provide credit enhancements, for example, default risk insurance. Some risk thus shifts from the security to the seller of insurance. Asset managers trade the securities. Servicers collect and make payments. Trustees of the special purpose vehicle monitor compliance with the legal and operating agreements (see figure 1 for a representation of the basic structure of securitization).

History and Recent Developments

Securitization in this form is just 40 years old[2]. It is an innovation by a government agency. In 1970 the U.S. Department of Housing and Urban Development created a mortgage-backed security. It was sold by the Government National Mortgage Association (GMNM or "Ginnie Mae"). In 1985 the first non-mortgage asset-backed security (ABS) was created by Marine Midland Bank – car loans.

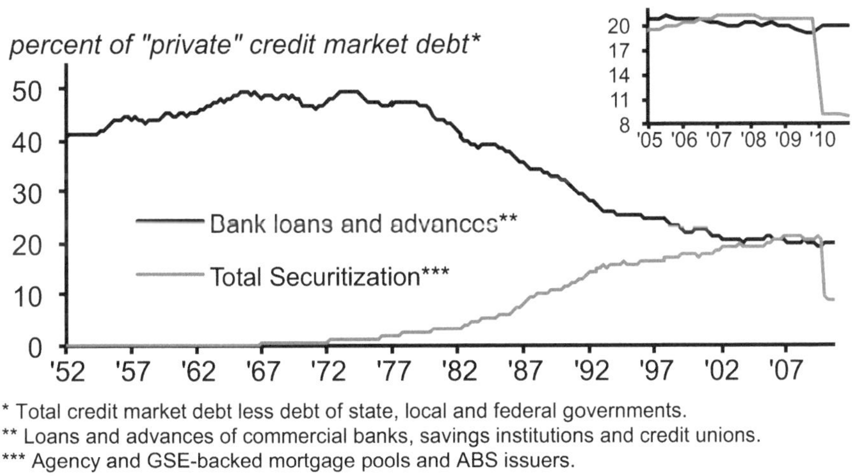

Fig. 2. Sources of credit in U.S.

Source: Institute for International Finance (2010)

[2] A very conservative form of pooling assets as collateral for bonds are so-called covered bonds, which have a 200 year history in Europe. However, in this case, the issuing institutions retain all risk on-balance sheet as opposed to "modern" securitization where risk is sold.

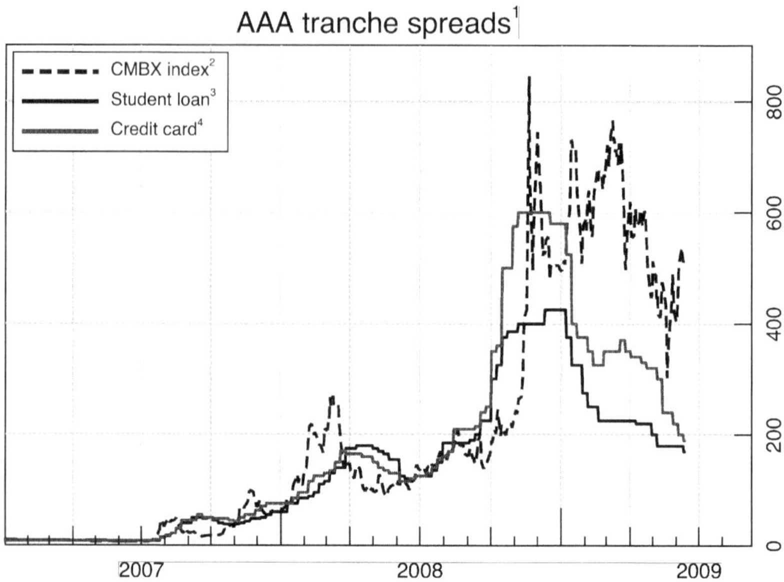

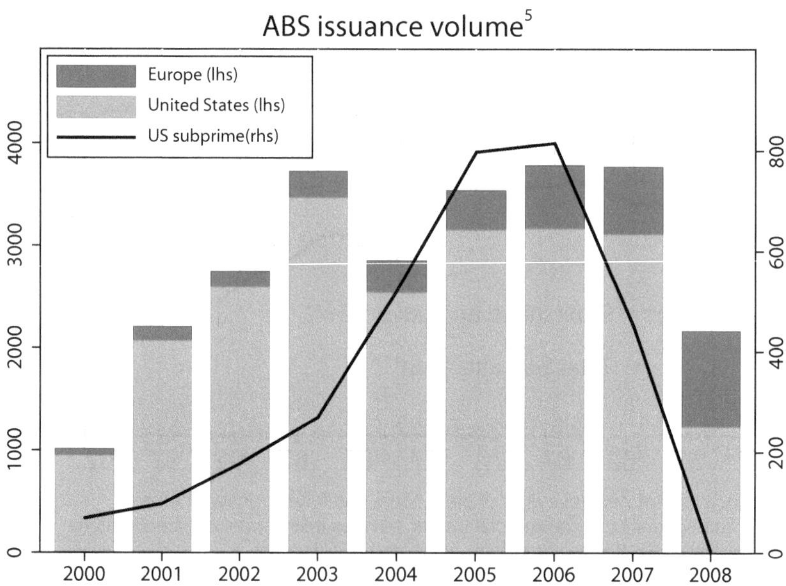

[1] In basis points. [2] Spreads on CDS index contracts referencing AAA-rated tranches of US commercial mortgage-backed securities (CMBX index, series 3). [3] Ten-year student loan ABS spreads to one-month Libor. [4] Ten-year floating credit card loan spreads to one-month Libor. [5] In billions of US dollars; includes agency and private label securitizations.

Fig. 3. Securitisation markets

Source: BIS (2009)

A year later came credit cards. In the 1990s securitization was applied to further markets including insurance markets.

During the last decade securitization became a greater source of credit for private borrowers than bank debt in the United States (figure 2). Private players became more prominent in securitization ("private-label securitization"). In 2005 and 2006 private label issuance outpaced that by government-sponsored agencies (Fannie Mae, Freddie Mac and Ginnie Mae) in the US. Private-label issuance peaked in the US in 2006 at well over $ 3 trillion. In Europe the private-label issuance peak was reached in 2008 with a bit over $ 1.2 trillion. Outside of the US and Europe private-label securitization took off in Australia, Canada, Japan and Korea and made modest progress in other markets, not least Latin America (IMF, 2009) with a peak issuance almost $ 0.4 trillion dollars in 2006. In mid 2008, just before the worst of the financial crisis, over $10 trillion of securitized assets were outstanding in the United States and well over $ 2 trillion in Europe.

In the run-up to the crisis issuance of mortgage-backed securities and related CDOs were the most "dynamic" part of the securitization market in the US and also Europe. When the crisis hit those parts of the market also suffered more than others (IMF, 2009 and figure 3).

While the market for low quality mortgages (sub-prime) and their securities collapsed most, even the best instruments were hit. Credit spreads rose dramatically even on AAA instruments, albeit a little less on credit card and student loan ABS than on MBS (figure 3). Once the crisis hit, private markets shut down almost completely. In the US, new issuance continued. Yet, it relied almost entirely on issues by U.S. government-sponsored agencies reaching about $ 1 trillion in 2009 (IMF, 2009). Private households among others sold such agency securities (figure 4). The Federal Reserve provided liquidity and bought them.

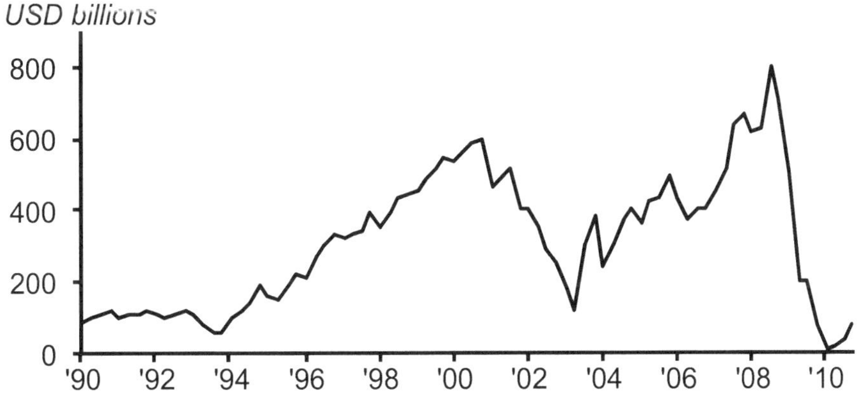

Fig. 4. U.S. household holdings of agency securities (holdings of agency- and GSE-backed securities by U.S. housholds and nonprofit organizations)

Source: Institute for International Finance (2010)

By the spring of 2010, private issuers started again cautiously to test the market. For example, Royal Bank of Scotland announced its intention to offer the first Commercial mortgage-based security since June 2008 backed by such assets as shopping malls and office buildings in the United States. It also became clearer that some classes of ABS had weathered the financial storms relatively well. The IMF's Global Financial Stability Report of April 2010 reported asset write-downs in US banks of over $ 200 billion for MBS, but zero for consumer-credit backed securities. Write-offs by European banks were estimated at close to $ 150 billion for MBS and just $ 8 billion for consumer-credit backed securities.

For now, the future of securitization remains uncertain. A large part of the MBS market continues to exist only because of government and central bank support. Multiple reform proposals in different jurisdictions cast uncertainty over the rules of the game. The fundamental question is whether it is worth preserving securitization at all.

The Promise of Securitization

In principle securitization can fulfill useful functions. Consider housing finance. For most people buying a house is the biggest financial transaction of a lifetime.[3] Houses are exceptionally long-lived assets. Most financing sources, however, are of much shorter duration. The trick then is to find a method of finance that can handle the risks arising from the maturity mismatch that is to some extent inevitable.

When banks issue mortgages with long maturities and fixed interest rates, they face interest rate risk. For example, the saving and loan (S&L) institution crisis in the United States exploded in the mid-1980s as S&Ls became unsustainable with deposit rates rising above the long-term rates on housing loans. If banks hedge the interest rate risk by offering adjustable rate mortgages, the borrower may not be able to pay the higher rate at some future date. While the interest rate risk looks hedged it has been transformed into credit risk of the borrower.

If banks or savings institutions had been able to create a form of mortgage finance that could have shifted some of the interest rate risk to investors with longer time horizons, the problems might have been more manageable. Securitization is a mechanism that makes mortgages tradable. They can thus be sold to investors who seek long-term assets to match long-term liabilities, such as pension funds and insurance companies, who on the other hand have no advantage in originating mortgages.

Tradability also means that a new store of value has been created for investors. As Jean Tirole has pointed out, this fits well with the view of Hernando de Soto

3 In most countries housing wealth is the biggest personal asset. Only in the United States and Belgium was financial wealth greater, in the former case presumably due to the stock market boom (Hellwig, 2008).

that a function of financial systems is to transform "dead capital" into "live capital" (Tirole, 2010).

More broadly, securitization is one way of allocating risks to those best able to manage or bear them. For example, junior tranches may suit distressed investors who can manage default situations, while senior tranches are attractive for investors that seek a particular set of maturity and yield combinations.

Moreover, MBS may allow diversification of idiosyncratic (non-system wide) risk, for example, shocks to income for a particular person or real estate prices in a particular area. In the US, Saving and Loan institutions were once obliged only to invest in "their community", in this case their state. When a shock hits a particular state, risks may become unmanageable. For example, when the oil price collapsed in 1985 it prompted the fall of house prices in Texas and led to the crisis of S&L institution in that state. In a global market, more idiosyncratic risk can, in principle, be diversified, for example, special shocks hitting whole countries or regions.

As with insurance products, pooling assets may help understand them better. Understanding the risks of an individual mortgage can be hard as it requires understanding the personal circumstances of the borrower. For a pool of mortgages that are issued on the basis of common underwriting standards, investors can analyze statistically the risks of default. They can thus gain greater comfort in understanding the performance of the average borrower than they could in understanding each individual borrower. To some degree, this argument is a variant of the diversification point. But beyond this, statistical analysis can at times teach the portfolio holder more about the average individual than those individuals know about themselves on average.

All in all, securitization has the potential to allocate risks in a more efficient manner. Access to finance may then expand and terms and conditions may improve as risks become more manageable. There is limited research on the impact of securitization on the economy overall. What exists suggests that securitization has the potential to expand access to finance and reduce spreads (Sabry and Okongwu, 2009).

The Dark Side of Securitization

The recent financial crisis has amply demonstrated that securitization can also entail major problems. Risks were apparently not allocated to those best able to bear or manage them, but, as the quip has it, to those least able to understand them. At the extreme, shoddy securities were created based on "NINJA" loans – loans for borrowers with "no income, no job and no assets". Nevertheless, the securities were made to look good and sold to investors who were willing to accept them despite low yields. Several questions arise. Why were substandard loans created? Why were they considered good and rated accordingly? Why did investors buy these products?

Consider first origination. With securitization, mortgages were largely not kept on the books of the originating institutions but sold to investors. This so-called "originate-distribute" model of finance has the potential to weaken the incentives of originators to adequately assess and manage the quality of mortgages. If originators had kept the junior tranches of securities on their books, they would typically have had the incentive to watch quality carefully. Yet, banks mostly sold off the junior tranches and kept senior tranches. The incentive of banks to do so is understandable. Shifting risk to others makes sense when the price of securities remains attractive, which it did. Regulatory obligations required banks to provide more capital for retained junior tranches than for higher quality tranches. This seems sensible. At the same time it can push banks to sell the junior tranches. To some degree regulatory arbitrage played a role. When banks placed junior tranches in a special vehicle that was "off-balance-sheet" and enhanced their quality through standby credit lines, regulation required lower minimum capital. Hence, the self-interest of originators and regulation both weakened the incentive to retain exposure to junior tranches.

Government policy also contributed to the creation of sub-standard products. Underwriting standards deteriorated for mortgages. For other securitizations such as credit cards reasonable standards appear to have been maintained. One reason was the push for access to housing finance in the United States. The government-sponsored agencies themselves ended up holding some $ 1 trillion of sub-prime mortgages (Calomiris, 2008) thus helping keep the price of securities up. Credit enhancements by the agencies provided comfort to investors despite underlying problems. The agencies themselves, while officially private, were de facto insured by taxpayers. In the face of rules and exhortations from policy-makers to expand access to finance to people with lower incomes, the agencies' own incentives and ability to maintain quality were weakened.

Not just originators sinned, but a number of participants in the whole process of assessing, selling and trading securitized products. Over time the quality of MBS weakened. Nevertheless, rating agencies provided good ratings. When the crisis hit ratings were downgraded in unprecedented ways suggesting that the original ratings were at best highly imprudent (IMF, 2009). Raters may have been lulled into a false sense of security, because country-wide house prices in the United States had not declined since World War II. Existing default histories showed little reason to be concerned. Yet, raters did not seem to question that existing default histories with limited time series might have been of little value and that house prices had risen to excessive levels compared to incomes. Also, the rating labels for securities meant something different than for corporate bonds. For example, as of 2005 Baa-rated CDOs had a five-year default probability of roughly 20% compared to about 2% for equally-rated corporate bonds (Calomiris, 2008).

When there are questions about the relevance of existing information a prudent assessor would discount the information and assign a conservative rating. Yet, rating agencies seem to have interpreted existing information in the best possible light rather than providing a more prudent assessment. They had incentives to do so, in part, because their consulting business depended on providing arrangers with advice on how to structure securitizations so as to achieve a desired rating. This may have led to "ratings-inflation". Being paid by arrangers rating agencies may also have an incentive to make things look as good as possible to help them sell the securities.

Asset managers and other participants in the sales process of securities kept offering low-quality products to investors, even when quality problems became more apparent.

A number of participants in the "agency-chain" from originator to final investor were paid fees for volume but were not exposed to losses or gains. Hence, their incentives were again to make things look as good as possible and sell as much as possible to maximize fee income. Others were paid bonuses as a function of current income or profit. They thus had incentives to use accounting treatments allowing the immediate recognition of income at the time of sale of a security. What happened later may have been of lesser concern.

All along the agency chain participants appear to have made use of all the possibilities to make securitized products looks as good as possible. They did not vigorously dispute questionable information, they exploited regulatory loopholes; they created products of exceptional complexity to make matters look better.[4]

It is not exactly surprising that lots of actors in the securitization process tried to make money and make products look as good as possible. This raises the most fundamental question. Why did investors buy low quality paper? And why did they buy low quality paper without requiring higher yield as compensation? In the years before the crisis, the spreads between yields on sub-prime and prime mortgages declined. Investors were thus willing to buy paper that became shoddier by the day for less of a premium.

It is not as if investors could not have known anything. As the quality of securities declined, newspapers and learned articles raised more and more questions about the sustainability of the housing boom and the quality of sub prime mortgages – before the crisis hit (Calomiris, 2008 and IMF 2009). Sophisticated investors could see all the assumptions underlying ratings. They could see that ratings for securitized paper meant something different than for corporate bonds. Even if they could not see everything, they should – as normal – have assumed that sellers have a natural incentive to make things look better than they are and discounted prices accordingly. Yet, they did the opposite. Prices were bid up and yield spreads declined.

Part of the reason may have been that even large sophisticated institutional investors may have imperfect incentives to watch over the interests of the final retail investor, contributors to insurance or pension schemes. They are remunerated on the basis of fund performance, but pay may not be always fully aligned with the

---

4 For example, an investor who would want to do due diligence on the quality of mortgages underlying a CDO-squared would need to go through about a billion pages of documents (Haldane, 2009).

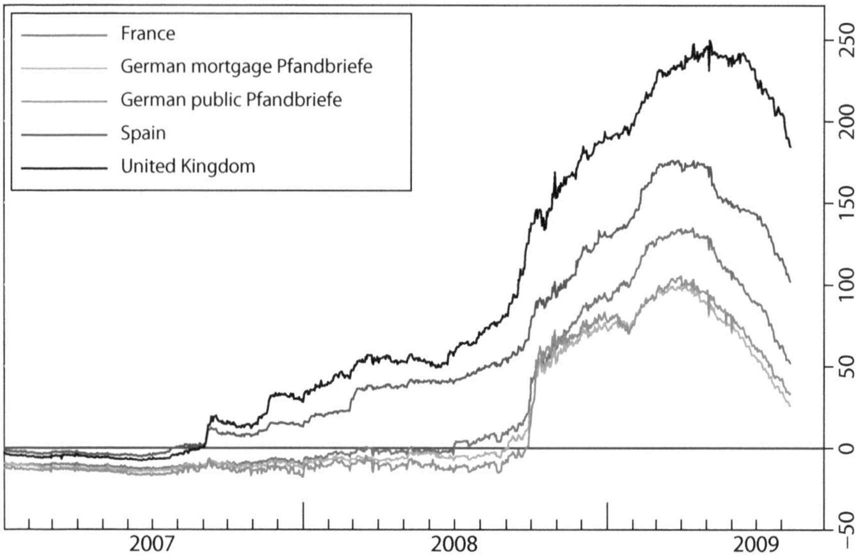

Fig. 5. Selected covered bond spreads (in basis points)
Source: IMF (2009)

long-term performance of investments. It is hard fully to align incentives as current performance is measurable, but long-term performance is still uncertain and one cannot practically postpone paying asset managers for too long.

A fundamental reason for the collapse of the securitization market seems to have been "excessive" liquidity instilling a "search for yield". Calomiris quotes the following event. A rating agency had not provided the rating that the sponsor wanted. As the sponsor turned to another agency, the "uninvited" agency warned a prominent institutional investor not to participate as a buyer. Yet, the investor ignored the warning saying "we have to put our money to work" (Calomiris, 2008). It was a time of ample liquidity when investors engaged in a search for yield and accepted even small margins over prime to buy sub prime.

To some degree excessive liquidity can arise due to self-reinforcing expectations about rising asset values, which allow greater borrowing, which in turn helps drive up asset prices. Loose monetary policy may also have been a contributor as short-term rates were very low, not only in the United States but globally (Borio, 2006). The boom faded as policy rates rose. Rates started rising in 2004. In the United States, by 2006, the peak of the boom, they had reached levels broadly consistent with the "Taylor Rule" that guides interest rate setting as a function of capacity utilization in an economy.

Importantly, in a boom it is hard to resist calls for more aggressive investment. This tendency afflicts financiers as well as politicians. Regulators and politicians have been pro-cyclical and not leaned against the boom. In normal times there may be wisdom in crowds, but in boom and busts the madness of crowds may dominate.

How a boom builds and collapses varies from crisis to crisis. In a boom, "water" (liquidity) may flow to those parts of the "dam" (underwriting and prudential standards) that have the most cracks – in this case the securitization market. Even so, some parts of the securitization market performed not too badly. Prime mortgage, credit card, car loan and student loan securitizations performed relatively well. "Covered bonds" proved their worth, particularly the tightly regulated German ones. These are securitized assets, where the originating bank retains full responsibility for a default and thus has the best conceivable incentives to be prudent. The weaknesses were most pronounced in the market for mortgages-backed securities, particularly the sub-prime market. That's where the dam burst.

The Future

Securitization holds promise. Some parts of the securitization system did not see a major erosion of underwriting standards. Covered bonds, the most conservative structure, have a 200 year history in Europe. Just as things look too rosy in a boom, they look to gloomy in a bust. Promising instruments that were once under cloud have made a comeback and are now accepted, notably "junk bonds". There is a future for securitization, but only with sensible standards, not as a wonder drug.

Regulatory reform proposals to render securitization more robust abound. They aim at improving the incentives of originators, typically through retention requirements, or at least disclosure of retention. Conflicts of interests of rating agencies and other incentive alignment problems are to be tackled. Finally, more disclosure on the quality of underlying assets is going to be required. Proposals vary across jurisdictions. The agenda remains unfinished.

The current regulatory uncertainty over the securitization process will delay the re-emergence of the market for securitized assets. Some overly complex instruments such as CDO-squared, the "financial alchemy" part of the market, may not make a comeback. In the end securitization should be more prudent and hence possibly less extensive. Covered bonds are emerging as an instrument of choice in Europe and Canada and are making an appearance in countries, where they were previously not used, such as Korea. In the first half of 2010 banks issued $ 210 billion of such bonds, more than the previous record of $ 204 billion in 2007[5]. However, in the US, as of the end of June 2010, the financial reform bill did not yet clarify critical legal issues required for the issuance of such bonds there[6].

For development finance it is sobering to see that attempts to expand access to finance, however well motivated, may backfire. More hard-headed credit and risk assessment may be required in areas such as securitization of microfinance assets.

---

[5] Financial Times, June 24, 2010.

[6] The Wall Street Journal, June 25, 2010.

There, maturity mismatch – one of the big arguments for securitization of housing finance – is not the issue. Being able to tap short-term finance, not least deposits, seems more promising. Exposure to foreign exchange risk in cross-border securitizations is also coming under greater scrutiny. Development of local bond and securitization markets will receive further attention.

Development finance is rightly concerned about access to finance. But what is the lasting good thing about access to finance? In many poor countries powerful elites have preferential access to finance. When people with sound credit, ideas or ventures can get financing – without powerful friends or relatives – incomes increase, inequality is reduced. When credit is granted without standards, crisis follows and poor people suffer.

Bibliography

Borio, C. (2006): "Monetary and Prudential Policies at a Crossroads? New Challenges in the New Century", BIS Working Paper No 216, September.

Calomiris, Charles W. (2008): "The Subprime Turmoil: What's Old, What's New, and What's Next", Paper presented at the 9th Jacques Polak Annual Research Conference, Washington D.C. November 13–14.

Fender, I.; Mitchell, J. (2009): "The future of securitization: how to align incentives?", BIS Quarterly Review, September .

Haldane, A. (2009): "Rethinking the Financial Network", Speech delivered at the Financial Student Association, Amsterdam, April.

Hellwig, M. (2008): "Systemic Risk in the Financial Sector: An Analysis of the Subprime-Mortgage Financial Crisis", Preprints of the Max Planck Institute for Research on Collective Goods 2008/43, Bonn, November.

Institute for International Finance (2010): "Capital Markets Monitor", Washington D.C. April.

International Monetary Fund (2009): "Global Financial Stability Report", Washington D.C., September.

International Monetary Fund (2010): "Global Financial Stability Report", Washington D.C., April.

Sabry, F.; Okongwu, C. (2009): "Study of the Impact of Securitization on Consumers, Investors, Financial Institutions and Capital Markets", NERA Economic Consulting.

Tirole, J. (2010): "Illiquidity and all its friends", BIS Working Paper No 303, Basel, March.

World Economic Forum (2006): "Building on the Monterrey Consensus: The untapped potential of development finance institutions to catalyze private investment", Geneva.

CHAPTER 2

Mobilising Capital for the Poor – How Does Structured Finance Fit in Emerging Markets?

Klaus Maurer[*]

Abstract

This paper examines the potential role of structured finance products for development finance. From the early experiences with structured transactions in microfinance, a number of open questions and issues are identified that need to be addressed for structured finance to play a significant role in development finance. In addition, and more fundamentally, the future outlook is overshadowed by the collapse of the global market for structured finance products in the aftermath of the subprime mortgage crisis in the USA. While the case for structured finance as an innovative financial technology remains strong, the structured finance market has serious structural problems that may be difficult – or take many years – to overcome. In that global context, it appears very challenging for structured finance to make a major inroad into development finance in the near future.

Introduction

This chapter provides an introduction and overview of structured finance and how it relates to development finance.

Historically, structured finance and development finance can be viewed as two distinct currents that have developed side by side in the ocean of global finance over the past decades. The origins of development finance date back to the establishment of the Bretton Woods institutions at the end of World War II. Structured finance evolved in the 1970s and 1980s, experienced a spectacular rise from 2000 to 2007 and an equally dramatic fall in 2008. In those boom years, a confluence of the two currents could be observed as structured finance began to emerge as an instrument for mobilising capital for development finance, and particularly for microfinance.

This chapter takes a closer look at this confluence of structured finance and development finance. It starts out with clarifying what structured finance is and how it has evolved primarily in the USA and in Europe. It then sketches the evolution of development finance over the past five decades and seeks to identify

[*] Consultant.

the role of structured finance in financial systems development. Finally, it addresses some of the key issues emerging from the early experiences before drawing final conclusions.

What Is Structured Finance?

There is no clear-cut definition of structured finance. Structured finance transactions often are – or appear – rather complex, involving many different parties. The development of structured finance was premised on credit being converted into a commodity. Hence, using an analogy with another commodity may illustrate its essential elements and characteristics.

The production, collection and processing of milk provides an illustrative example.[1] Milk is produced by dairy farms following defined standards, and is then collected and processed. Milk processing entails separation, standardisation, pasteurisation and homogenisation. Through this process, raw milk with an average fat content of between 4% and 6% is converted into dairy products with different fat contents. A low fat segment with a maximum fat content of 2% comprises skimmed and low fat milk. A medium fat group (fat content of 2% to 35%) includes whole milk, yoghurt and cream. Finally, a high fat segment (35% to over 80%) includes dairy products like cheese and butter.

Structured finance follows the same principles. Financial assets, such as loans or credit card receivables, and future flows such as telephone payments or remittances from workers abroad are treated as a commodity. Securitisation provides the method to create the pools of assets or future flows that are used in the creation of different classes or tranches of securities. In the process, the risk inherent in credits is being professionally measured and rated. As a logical follow-up, if the risk could be measured and traded as a commodity with the underlying financing involved, the financing and the credit could be stripped as two different products.

The essence of structured finance is capital market-based risk transfer. A broad definition is provided by Jobst[2]: Structured finance encompasses all advanced private and public financial arrangements that serve to efficiently refinance and hedge any profitable economic activity beyond the scope of conventional forms of on-balance sheet securities (debt, bonds, equity) in the effort to lower the cost of capital and to mitigate the agency costs of market impediments on liquidity. Accordingly, structured finance products can be broken down into (i) asset securitisation for refinancing and (ii) credit derivatives for hedging.

The Committee on the Global Financial System (2005) defines structured finance more narrowly based on three characteristics that tend to be associated more specifically with securitisation:

---

[1] The analogy is taken from Alessandro Tappi, EIF, from a presentation at the EFSE Annual Meeting 2007 in Budva, Montenegro.

[2] Jobst, Andreas A. (2006): Sovereign securitization in emerging markets. In: Journal of Structured Finance, Vol.12, No.3, p. 3.

> *Structured finance instruments can be defined through three key characteristics:*
>
> *(1) pooling of assets (either cash-based or synthetically created),*
>
> *(2) tranching of liabilities that are backed by the asset pool [...],*
>
> *(3) delinking of the credit risk of the collateral asset pool from the credit risk of the originator, usually through the use of a finite-lived stand alone special purpose vehicle (SPV).*

Securitisation is the structured process whereby interests in loans and other receivables are packaged, underwritten, and sold in the form of asset-backed securities. Initially, securitisation served as a *regulatory arbitrage tool* but developed into an efficient and flexible funding and capital management technique.[3] Today, for many institutions it serves as an effective *balance sheet management tool.*[4] The advantages for the originators have included the relief in regulatory and economic capital, access to new and cheaper sources of funding, and portfolio management. Investors' interest has been primarily motivated by portfolio diversification and attractive risk-return profiles.

Structured Finance Products

There are several main types of structured finance instruments and products. *Asset-backed securities (ABS)* are bonds or notes based on pools of assets, or collateralised by the cash flows from a homogeneous granular (i.e. small ticket) pool of underlying financial assets. These assets consist of residential or commercial mortgages, consumer and auto loans, credit card receivables or small and medium-sized enterprise (SME) loans. They are priced by means of a statistical migration analysis. *Collateralised debt obligations (CDO)* consolidate a group of heterogeneous, bulky, fixed income assets into a pool, which is then divided into various tranches. They can be created prior to, or as a result of, the transaction and are priced with traditional corporate rating methods. *Credit derivatives* are contracts to transfer the risk of the total return on a credit asset from falling below an agreed level, without transfer of the underlying asset. These pure credit derivatives include, for example, Credit Default Swaps (CDS) and Total Return Swaps (TRS). Relatively new phenomena are *Structured Investment Funds* which use elements of structured finance such as pooling of assets and tranching of securities. An example is the European Fund for Southeast Europe (EFSE)[5] promoted by KfW.

---

3 Jobst, Andreas A. (2006): Sovereign securitization in emerging markets. In: Journal of Structured Finance 12(3), op. cit. pp. 2–13.

4 Basu, Sudiptu (2005): Securitization and the Challenges Faced in Micro Finance. Center for Microfinance Research Working Paper Series. April 2005.

5 For more information about EFSE refer to www.efse.lu.

Origins and Evolution of Structured Finance

Securitisation began in the **United States** with the structured financing of mortgage pools in 1970, when the Government National Mortgage Association (GNMA or *Ginnie Mae*) created the first transaction and sold securities backed by a portfolio of mortgage loans. In the mid-eighties, securitisation techniques that had been developed in the mortgage market were applied for the first time to non-mortgage assets: a USD 60 million securitisation of automobile loans originated by Marine Midland Bank in 1985 and the first significant bank credit card sale with a private placement of US$ 50 million. Since then, securitisation has become one of the largest sources of debt financing in the US with an estimated total aggregate outstanding of USD 8 trillion as of the end of 2005, representing about 30% of the total outstanding US bond market. Securitisation reached its peak in 2006 with the issuance of nearly USD 1 trillion in mortgage bonds during that year. This was shortly before the outbreak of the subprime mortgage crisis in mid-2007.

In **Europe**, securitisation began in 1986 in the UK with the first mortgage-backed security (MBS) issue. In the following two decades, the market has grown rapidly and in 2006, Europe recorded a volume of Euro 542 billion (Euro 384 billion in 2005). The UK has the largest market with a share of 35%, followed by Spain 12%, Netherlands 11% and Germany 10%.

Securitisation has also assumed a vital role in **emerging market economies** since the end of the 1980s, especially in large countries like Mexico or India. Future flow securitisation (FFS) debuted in Mexico when Teléfonos de México S.A. de C.V. securitised its telephone receivables in 1987. Since then, large and highly-rated corporates and banks in developing economies have successfully sold receivables from future claims against obligors. In India, the first securitisation occurred in 1991 with auto loan receivables. Fifteen years later, there have been 123 issuances with over USD 7 billion in one year.

The US Subprime Crisis and the Collapse of Structured Finance Market

Developments changed fundamentally with the outbreak of the subprime mortgage crisis in the USA in mid-2007 which rapidly expanded to the global credit markets. Within less than one year by mid-2008, the structured finance activity was effectively shut down.

Initially, the crisis unfolded as a liquidity crisis in summer 2007. The off-balance sheet vehicles of commercial banks were heavily exposed to maturity mismatch, because long-term assets (mortgage loans) have been refinanced by short-term commercial papers. Through granting liquidity backstops to their off-balance sheet vehicles, the commercial banks came under considerable financial stress when investors stopped buying short-term papers.[6]

---

6 See Brunnermeier, Markus (2009): Deciphering the Liquidity and Credit Crunch 2007–2008. In: Journal of Economic Perspectives 23, Winter 2009.

Following the collapse of the market, a number of structural problems and flaws of structured finance became apparent. It is beyond the scope of this paper to present a comprehensive analysis. Hence, only some key points are listed in the following:

- The asset-backed securities were held in **off-balance sheet vehicles**, as Special Purpose Vehicles (SPV), outside the regulatory and supervisory framework. When the securities had to be taken on balance sheet in the unfolding crisis, the banks proved to be highly undercapitalized.
- The structures were highly complex and investors relied entirely on the **rating agencies' assessments**. Providing triple-A-ratings allowed trillions of dollars of risky assets to be transformed into securities that were widely considered to be 'safe'. However, a huge portion of the triple-A-rated tranches was downgraded to "junk" in the course of the crisis.
- Too little attention was paid to the **conflict of interest** that arose, because the rating agencies were providing consulting services on the very things that they were also rating.
- The **complex rating models** for structured finance products were extremely fragile. A slight mistake or a modest imprecision in evaluating underlying risks could easily jeopardize the rating result. In several instances, rating agencies confirmed flaws and bugs in their models. In addition, there is a tendency of pooling and tranching to amplify the mistakes in the default risk assessment and correlations.[7]
- Structured finance products are highly exposed to **systemic risk** because the performance of securities created by tranching large asset pools is strongly affected by the performance of the economy as a whole. This fact was neither reflected in the rating models nor in the pricing of securities and tranches.[8]
- Asset origination was severely affected by **moral hazard**. Because the institutions responsible for origination did not hold any equity shares, they did not have much of an incentive to take care in borrower creditworthiness assessments. They were more interested in volume than in quality control.[9] As a consequence, underwriting standards deteriorated significantly.

---

7 See Coval, Joshua D., Jakub Jurek, Erik Stafford (2008): The Economics of Structured Finance. Working Paper 09-060. Harvard Business School.

8 Ibid, p. 8.

9 See Hellwig, Martin (2008): Systemic Risk in the Financial Sector: An Analysis of the Subprime-Mortgage Financial Crisis. Max Planck Institute for Research on Collective Goods, Bonn.

These structural and fundamental problems need to be addressed before the market for structured finance products will likely recover. The US structured finance market has somewhat stabilized in 2009 and will likely continue to stabilize in 2010 but the commercial mortgage-backed securities (CMBS) market remains a concern (Standard & Poor's 2010). New issuances have been rare and are likely to remain modest for some time to come.

Mobilising Capital for the Poor: The Evolving Viewpoint of Development Finance

Mobilising capital for the poor has been a key area in development finance for the past four decades. Today's viewpoint has evolved over time and has gone through stages which are briefly recalled in this section.

1960–70s: Supply-Led Finance

In its early days, development finance was based on the belief that developing countries suffered from a saving and investment gap. The nations were considered too poor to generate a surplus resulting in a low level of investment, that in turn lead to low employment and low income levels: a vicious circle. The appropriate response was thought to be capital transfers from industrial countries to propel investments. State-owned agricultural and industrial development banks were established to channel official aid funds to predefined sectors and target groups, primarily farmers and industrial enterprises. This was the era of supply-led finance.

1980s: Failure of Development Banks; Emergence of Microfinance

After less than two decades, most development banks were confronted with massive loan defaults and losses which finally led many to fail and close. The model of state-owned development banks channelling exclusively public funds was declared bankrupt by the World Bank and the donor community in 1989. A few development banks were successfully reformed, e.g. BRI Indonesia and BAAC Thailand.

The same period witnessed the emergence of early initiatives in microfinance led by non-governmental organisations (NGOs) and their networks in Latin America, e.g. ACCION in Bolivia, and in Asia, e.g. Grameen Bank in Bangladesh. Initially funded by welfare organisations, these microfinance institutions were increasingly supported by donors and public funds, mostly on a grant basis.

1990s: Mainstreaming and Commercialisation of Microfinance; Downscaling of Commercial Banks; Financial Systems Development

The initiatives of 1990s focused on the mainstreaming and increasing commercialisation of microfinance. The result was a considerable number of established and successful MFIs (microfinance institutions) around the world that grew substantially, produced consistent and significant profits, accumulated assets in the form of micro-loans with relatively low default and loss rates. Top tier MFIs became rated and established track records with lenders. Some MFIs transformed into regulated financial institutions which allowed them to mobilise deposits, but most remained dependent on donor or public funding. In the same period, "down-scaling" of commercial banks produced successful results. Many small and local commercial banks began to lend to SME and for housing.

Most donors and international agencies realigned their strategies under a comprehensive financial systems development approach. Financial intermediation became the centrepiece of this approach where the mobilisation of *private* capital and *domestic* resources received particular emphasis. At the end of the 1990s, development finance became synonymous with financial systems development.

Since 2000: Building Inclusive Financial Systems; Massive Upscaling of Microfinance

The UN Millennium Development Goals – eradicating poverty, providing decent housing, etc. – gave another boost to development finance. Development finance as currently understood encompasses microfinance, rural finance, SME finance, housing finance, infrastructure and municipal finance, and most recently fields like energy efficiency and environmental finance, all against the background of the debate on climate change.

Given the masses of people at the "bottom of the pyramid" without access to formal financial services, access to finance has become the imperative for policy makers and development agencies like the World Bank. To achieve these goals, massive efforts are essential and there is a wide consensus in the development community that scarce public funds supporting a few institutions will not and cannot fill this gap. Adopting a more commercial approach involving private capital and the capital markets – in partnership with public sector institutions – is the only way to reach the scale envisaged. Efforts must be directed towards building inclusive financial systems focused on institution building and capacity development, including the development of local capital markets. A strong base of local financial institutions able to serve the intended target groups should be developed, including local commercial banks, credit unions and cooperatives (especially in rural areas), microfinance banks and other non-bank financial institutions.

Microfinance is the key approach in responding to those conditions. The sector has grown tremendously in the past few years. It has seen the transformation and establishment of specialised microfinance banks (ACLEDA, XAC, BancoSol, ProCredit, Opportunity, K-REP, etc.) and the increasing integration of microfinance into the mainstream financial system. The microfinance banks increasingly rely on domestic deposits as their main funding source. However, the loan portfolio growth of most institutions outpaces their capacity to mobilise local funds, increasing the gap between the demand and supply of refinance. The refinancing of the global microfinance sector has fostered the emergence of socially responsible and commercial microfinance investment funds and vehicles (MIVs). In 2008, 103 MIVs were operating in the sector with estimated USD 6.6 billion assets under management.[10]

The year of microcredit in 2005 and the award of the Nobel Prize to Mohammad Yunus and the Grameen Bank have further fuelled investors' interest. The challenge for a new generation of microfinance investment is to structure microfinance investments that provide MFIs with efficient access to a broader investor base.

Financing gaps prevail in areas other than microfinance. As domestic capital markets in many developing countries are absent or highly underdeveloped, medium to long term capital is scarce. This prevents local financial institutions from providing medium to long term loans for capital investments in the small and medium enterprise sectors and for housing and mortgages. Despite the considerable liquidity of local financial institutions in many emerging markets, a maturity gap exists for medium and long tenors.

Role of Structured Finance for Financial Systems Development

Initial Structured Finance Transactions in Development Finance

Structured finance transactions have played an increasing role in emerging market countries since the late 1980s. Prominent examples are large countries such as Mexico, Argentina and India which have engaged in securitisation of telephone receivables, auto loans and mortgages. However, few of those transactions were geared to development finance in a narrow sense.

Development finance has included structured finance operations only in the early years of the new century. Most of these early transactions were related to microfinance.[11] The majority of deals, including the BlueOrchard BOMFS/BOLD, Global partnerships and the most recent Deutsche Bank/KfW db Microfinance Invest Nr. 1, comprised CDOs of loans to, or purchase of notes of MFIs in various countries as second-tier transactions or indirect securitisation. Furthermore, structured investment funds such as EFSE or the Regional Microfinance Fund for Africa (REGMIFA) have been established with a development mission.

First-tier transactions or direct securitisation of loans to end users have been few. Only a limited number of microcredit SME securitisations have been undertaken: ProCredit Bulgaria and Serbia[12] as well as BRAC[13] in Bangladesh.

Early experience with structured finance has faced a number of challenges:

---

[10] For more information see CGAP 2009 MIV benchmark survey.

[11] See an overview of deal profiles in the Annex.

[12] For more information about ProCredit Bulgaria and Serbia refer to www.procredit-bank.bg/main/en/ and www.procreditbank.bg/main/en/.

[13] For more information about BRAC refer to www.brac.net/.

- *The variety of microfinance lending methodologies:* In most countries a range of lending methodologies exist – such as solidarity group loans, village banking and individual loans with many variations. Only when many MFIs make substantially similar loans using similar legal frameworks and underwriting standards can a true market in securitised microloans be contemplated.
- *Country risk:* The benefit of a potentially low microloan credit risk is often diminished by the country risk of an MFI's country of origin. This may be addressed by diversification in the form of a multi-country transaction, which would however tremendously increase complexity.
- *Legal framework:* A cash securitisation transaction would most probably have to be structured with an on-shore SPV. This may raise legal issues such as the availability of a functioning securitisation framework. Main legal issues to be addressed are notification requirements (if any) for the huge number of assets to be transferred and the bankruptcy-remoteness of the securitisation vehicle.
- *Tax issues:* Servicing costs for microloans are much higher than for traditionally securitised assets. If servicing cost, which is the fee paid to the servicer when the assets are securitised, becomes subject to VAT, the transaction may be materially affected.

For all of the above reasons, most investments involve pooled loans to MFIs rather than pooling the underlying loans to microentrepreneurs for securitisation.

The outbreak of the subprime crisis and the collapse of the global market for structured finance products led to a complete standstill of structured transactions in the area of development finance. Despite the growing popularity of microfinance as an asset class for conventional investors, no further securitisations or CDOs were structured from 2007 to date.

Potential Benefits of Structured Finance for Local Financial Institutions

From the perspective of local financial institutions as originators, there are three reasons for engaging in structured finance transactions: (i) access to refinance from capital markets, (ii) transfer of risk and (iii) regulatory restrictions.

(i) Access to Refinance from Capital Markets: Structured finance enables local financial institutions to gain access to new (and often cheaper) sources of funding from domestic or international capital markets, even for unrated institutions. Through structured finance products, microfinance institutions can especially broaden their investor base to more commercial and financially motivated investors, thereby matching the various types of investors' risk/return profiles.

(ii) Transfer of Risk: The transfer of risk to the capital market is the essence of asset securitisation. First, such transfer allows a financial institution to manage exposure limits that may be in place for certain economic sectors, regions or client groups. Second, risk transfer provides capital relief. Most regulated financial institutions are bound by capital adequacy requirements. Due to partial or total removal of assets from their balance sheet in a true sale securitisation, the reduction of regulatory and sometimes economic capital can be significant. However, the other side of the coin is the potential risk of reduced portfolio quality: if only good risks are securitised, a concentration of bad risks may remain with the originator.

(iii) Overcoming Regulatory Restrictions: In some jurisdictions, lending restrictions can constrain local financial institutions: a transfer of loans may mitigate such a constraint. An example is the ProCredit Bulgaria securitisation which was primarily motivated by lending restrictions required by the central bank. The restrictions were imposed for monetary policy reasons, i.e. to curb consumer credit growth, but their broad brush nature had serious side effects on lending to enterprises and the productive sector. Hence, the transaction was supported by the central bank.

It should be noted that the latter two benefits only materialize in first-tier transactions, i.e. direct securitisations, while the rationale for participating in second-tier transactions such as global CDOs is confined to access to refinancing from capital markets.

Rationale of Structured Finance for Financial Systems Development

From the perspective of financial systems development, there are at least three potential roles for structured finance.

The prime rationale of structured finance is the **mobilisation of private capital** for lending to microenterprises, farmers, SMEs, for housing purposes, and for filling gaps between supply and demand.

A second rationale is the leverage of scarce public funds. In structured finance transactions, public funds are strategically employed as a junior or first loss tranche, a guarantee or other form of credit enhancement. Public institutions including the Development Finance Institutions (DFIs) can serve as *lead or anchor investors*. Through subordination in a public private partnership, public money functions as a catalyst to attract private capital, especially in areas where private capital alone would not otherwise go. Moreover, scarce public funds can be freed and allocated to new financial institutions, supporting next tier financial institutions, funding innovations and reducing market inefficiencies.

A third rationale is the development of local capital markets and linking them to the international capital markets. A structured finance transaction can contribute to creating a local investor base. For example, in the BRAC Bangladesh securitisation, the senior tranche was placed with local investors. Furthermore, an early structured finance transaction may be a prime mover, fostering the creation of the necessary legal and regulatory framework. In Bulgaria, the ProCredit Bank securitisation was the first to provide an example. Creating links to the international capital markets is equally important, for example through participation in global CDOs.

However, these potential benefits of structured finance are overshadowed by a number of structural problems and shortcomings which surfaced in the wake of the financial crisis and led to the collapse of the market for structured finance products. More than two years after the outbreak of the crisis, it is unclear whether and how the market can be revived.

Open Questions and Critical Issues

The application of structured finance products in the context of development finance lasted a short period. These early experiences have raised a number of questions and issues around the role of structured finance for the development agenda of building inclusive financial systems. Some of the key points are discussed in the following.

Structured Finance: Substitute or Complement to Domestic Savings Mobilisation?

Critics of structured finance applications in developing countries argue that it undermines domestic savings mobilisation. Some fear that an abundance of debt capital could distract local financial institutions from mobilising savings.

This concern may be valid for banks and other deposit-taking institutions. It certainly does apply to specialised lending institutions, mostly non-bank financial institutions (NBFIs) such as mortgage and leasing companies, and for those MFIs that are not permitted to mobilise deposits. These institutions obtain refinancing from creditors and capital markets.

But even for deposit-taking institutions, there is a rationale for external refinance to manage the maturity gap. Deposits are short-term by nature due to customer preferences and sometimes due to banking regulations. For example, in Russia and Ukraine, depositors have the right to withdraw their deposits at any time, irrespective of the contract term. Hence, from a risk point of view, all deposits are short term. Given the regulatory restrictions on term transformation in most countries, deposits can mostly be used for short-term loans, e.g. consumer loans or working capital. Structured finance offers long-term refinancing for fixed asset investments or mortgage lending. Different products and market segments are served by different funding sources.

From a financial system perspective, structured finance and external refinancing can be complementary to domestic savings mobilisation under two conditions: a) funds are provided to non-deposit-taking institutions, and b) if they are provided to deposit-taking institutions they have a medium to long tenor dedicated to medium to long term loans, or the loan growth in such institutions is faster than deposit growth.

Domestic Versus International Transactions: What Is the Right Balance?

The majority of the transactions have been international. On the asset side, loans to financial institutions are pooled across countries, and on the liability side bonds and notes are placed with international capital markets. As noted, there have been few domestic transactions.

Critics have raised concerns about this approach. The first concern is about foreign currency denominated loans to local financial institutions whose lending business is primarily in local currency (microfinance, SME, housing). Euro or US Dollar loans tend to be appealing, because they usually carry a nominally lower interest rate than local currency loans. However, unless hedged, the foreign exchange risk remains with the local financial institution or is passed on to the final borrowers. The second concern is that – by placing securities with international investors – development finance will be exposed to the volatility of international capital markets. The third point is that country risk limits the rating of the securities: this would not be a restriction, if securities were placed with local investors.

These critics clearly favour domestic transactions which – in addition to the above – provide further benefits. First, the magnitude of funds raised is appropriate for local financial institutions. Second, domestic transactions would foster first-tier transactions, i.e. securitisations of end user loan portfolios instead of loans to financial institutions. Third, domestic transactions would address local investors looking for good investment opportunities. For example, pension funds in Eastern Europe are required to invest in highly-rated securities which normally are scarce within their own country. Their presence significantly contributes to the development of local capital markets. Finally, domestic transactions would strengthen local financial intermediation.

The proponents of international transactions maintain that through these transactions local institutions and markets are connected to international capital markets. Moreover, by creating international asset pools across regions, risks are diversified and the structure becomes more stable. They emphasise the demonstration effect that an international transaction may have on local markets. Finally, they point to the fact that many countries' legal frameworks are not yet sufficient for structuring a domestic transaction.

From the perspective of financial systems development, domestic transactions should be the primary goal for all the reasons mentioned earlier: promoting local currency intermediation, serving local investors, avoiding country rating ceiling limits, helping create the legal framework and the development of local capital markets. However, international transactions will continue to play an important and complementary role in linking domestic and international capital markets.

Size and Scale: How Can Structured Finance Be Downscaled to Serve Smaller Financial Institutions?

Securitisations often require large scale structuring and minimum volume thresholds which are beyond the absorption capacity of a single local financial institution. A securitisation may not be cost-efficient for small and medium-sized transactions. This is particularly relevant for MFIs where large numbers of borrowers but small volumes of money define the business model. Size and scale considerations have quite likely been the rationale for pooling several MFIs in one transaction. Critics point out that most of the CDOs have primarily worked with top-tier, high-performing MFIs such as the early BlueOrchard transactions. Expanding the outreach to the broader microfinance industry would require a "downscaling" of structured finance to serve smaller and riskier MFIs.

Complexity and Cost: When Does Structured Finance Pay Off?

Small volumes translate into high transaction costs. Securitisations are expensive and the more complex, the more expensive they are. Costs are related to management and systems, including underwriting fees, rating fees, and ongoing administration. Critics argue that structured finance is too sophisticated and complex for development finance, given the small scale of institutions and the small underlying loan sizes. For example, MFIs may need to pool ten to fifty thousand microloans to create an investment large enough to interest investors. In most transactions, the size of the first loss tranche has been relatively high, increasing the funding cost.

But despite high transaction costs, several transactions have taken place. The proponents of structured finance take a different view on transaction costs. First, the application of structured finance transactions in development finance is new and there is an initial learning curve for all parties. This cost will decline as participants become more familiar with systems and procedures. For example, the size of the first loss tranche declined to less than 7% in the 2007 db Microfinance Invest Nr. 1 transaction. Second, transaction costs must be seen as investments in the long run: they will decline considerably with repeated transactions. Third, the transaction costs for an investor in a structured finance transaction may be lower than for a lender in conventional refinance, although a full comparative cost analysis remains to be conducted. Fourth, transaction costs are lowered when creditors in conventional refinance such as DFIs become investors in structured finance transactions.

The challenges for arrangers and structuring institutions lie in reducing the complexity of transactions, aligning transaction costs with deal sizes – in line with downscaling as mentioned above – and increasing cost efficiency. The number of parties involved in highly specialised functions may have to be reduced in small-scale transactions. Specific features of development finance may have to be taken into account when structuring a transaction. For example, the credit risk of microloans is closely linked to the servicer. This means that isolating the microloan credit risk from the originator/servicer counterparty risk is difficult to achieve. The role of a back-up servicer may require modification in securitised microloans.

Impact of Structured Finance: How to Maximise the Benefit for the End Users?

Development finance is concerned with the impact on the end users. This question gains relevance when donors or DFIs are involved in structured finance transactions, e.g. through participation in higher risk tranches or through credit enhancements. How is it possible to determine and measure the impact of structures that are increasingly remote from the final users? What are the benefits of structured finance transactions for the ultimate borrowers, the micro and small entrepreneurs, the homeowners? To what extent are cost savings and efficiency gains passed on to final borrowers? Thorny questions such as these, call for answers before development finance can fully embrace structured finance. The pictures and tragic stories of low-income Americans facing foreclosure of their homes in the aftermath of the subprime crisis strengthen the critics rather than the proponents of structured finance.

Conclusion and Outlook

The discussion brings us back to the original question: What can structured finance contribute to mobilising capital for the poor?

Structured finance – as an innovative financial technology – may be appealing from a public policy point of view, because it offers a smart approach to leveraging scarce public funds. It links development finance with private investors and capital markets, and offers scope for the massive upscaling in financial services that is necessary to achieve the Millennium Development Goals.

Building inclusive financial systems entails mobilising capital for the poor on a *sustainable* basis. In the medium and long run, this will be ensured by domestic savings mobilisation and the development of local capital markets. International refinance will play an important role in bridging the gaps until local financial systems can assume the primary role. In view of the massive scale and volumes required, structured finance may provide a mechanism for bringing in private investors and capital markets, in ways complementary and additional to domestic savings mobilisation. In view of local capital market development, domestic structured finance transactions are the preferred choice. These would entail transactions in appropriate scale and volume, at reasonable transaction costs, structured in local currency, creating the legal and regulatory framework as well as mobilising local investors.

The overriding and fundamental questions, however, remain: Can the market for structured finance products recover? Can structured finance be reformed and its structural flaws eliminated? Some practitioners believe that that the crisis will work itself out and the market for structured finance will return as before. Others hold the more sceptical view that the market for structured finance products has serious structural problems that may be difficult to overcome.[14]

While the intellectual case for structured finance – as an innovative financial technology – remains strong, it may take many years to solve the structural problems and to remove the uncertainties which are currently prevailing in the global market for structured finance products. Under these overarching conditions, it appears unlikely for structured finance to make a major inroad into development finance in the foreseeable future.

References

Basu, Sudiptu (2005): Securitization and the Challenges Faced in Micro Finance. Center for Microfinance Research Working Paper Series, April 2005.

Brunnermeier, Markus (2009): Deciphering the Liquidity and Credit Crunch 2007–2008. In: Journal of Economic Perspectives 23, Winter 2009.

Committee on the Global Financial System (2005): The role of ratings in structured finance: issues and implications. Bank for International Settlements. January 2005.

Coval, Joshua D.; Jurek, Jakub; Stafford, Erik (2008): The Economics of Structured Finance. Working Paper 09-060. Harvard Business School.

Jobst, Andreas A. (2006): Sovereign securitization in emerging markets. In: Journal of Structured Finance 12(3), pp. 2–13.

Jobst, Andreas A. (2007): A primer on structured finance. In: Journal of Derivatives and Hedge Funds 13(3).

Jung, Philipp; Eriksson, Per-Erik (2006): Microfinance loan obligations – Structured Finance for Microfinance Investments. In: Robbé and Ali (eds): Innovation in Securitization Yearbook 2006.

Hellwig, Martin (2008): Systemic Risk in the Financial Sector: An Analysis of the Subprime-Mortgage Financial Crisis. Max Planck Institute for Research on Collective Goods. Bonn.

Mitchell, Janet (2005): Financial Intermediation Theory and implications for the sources of value in structured finance markets. National Bank of Belgium. Working paper document No. 71.

The Economist (2009): Rebuilding the banks. A special report on international banking. May 14th, 2009.

World Economic Forum (2006): Blended value investing: Capital opportunities for social and environmental impact. March 2006.

[14] See Coval, Joshua D., Jakub Jurek and Erik Stafford (2008): The Economics of Structured Finance. Working Paper 09-060. Harvard Business School.

CHAPTER 3

The Role of Public and Private Investors for Structured Finance in Emerging Markets

Peter Hartig[*]

Abstract

This chapter presents the different roles and contributions of the main actors of structured finance (SF) transactions in development finance, namely donors, development finance institutions (DFI) and private investors (PI). We present in a simplified manner the different risk-return profiles and the resulting contributions of the various actors to successful SF deals. The paper analyses the interplay of the various actors based on empirical evidence. SF transactions in development finance are rapidly changing, reflecting changing behaviour and risk perceptions by the various players. However, structural differences between public and private stakeholders remain. At least for the time being public investors are needed to bridge private investors into markets and new asset classes in emerging market countries.

Introduction

SF seems to emerge as an attractive instrument to mobilise sustainable capital from a broad range of local and international commercial investors who want to finance pro-poor assets in emerging market countries. New asset classes and markets consist of micro and small and medium-sized enterprise (SME) loans, low-cost housing portfolios, municipal lending and loans for environmental investments. Besides improving access to funds for the banks involved, SF offers additional developmental advantages by using limited public resources to leverage private investors. This contributes to local financial sector and capital market development and to the integration of domestic financial systems into international capital markets.[1]

Compared to more traditional methods of financing (e.g. plain debt, equity)[2], SF is considered superior in its capacity to align banks' and private investors'

[*] Consultant.

[1] However, during the recent financial and economic crisis this integration has proven as a factor of instability.

[2] It should be noted that deposits are still the major source for financing of many MFIs.

interests. This chapter discusses how this alignment is achieved, what hurdles have to be removed and what roles the different stakeholders can play. A main issue is the extent to which public sector investors are needed to bring private investors into markets in emerging market countries

We then provide a rather simplified categorisation of the different risk-return profiles and roles of the various SF stakeholders. The types of SF transactions in development finance and in the market are rapidly changing reflecting changing behaviour and risk perception of the various players in each deal.

This chapter highlights structural differences between public and private stakeholders' roles. It briefly describes the basic structure of a transaction, possible stakeholders and their respective roles and contributions; explains the interplay of the various actors in SF based on empirical evidence; and provides a summary that offers the main conclusions.

Basic SF Structure and Stakeholders

Major actors in a SF transaction are the originator, the servicer (often the originator), the arranger, the guarantor (enhancer) and the investors.[3] Examples of different types of originators in emerging market countries are microfinance institutions (MFIs), SME banks and banks with environmental and low-cost housing portfolios.[4]

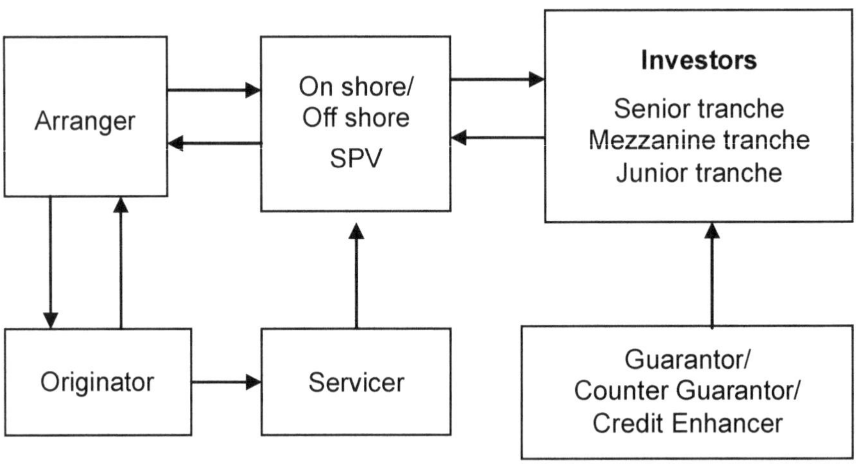

Fig. 1. Basic structure of SF-transactions

---

[3] See figure 1.

[4] For simplicity the term "banks" is used for all these different types of financial institutions in emerging markets, including non-bank microfinance institutions such as NGOs or finance companies.

The servicer, who may also be the arranger, manages the asset pool on behalf of the Special Purpose Vehicle (SPV) created for the securitization. The task of the arranger is to structure the deal, negotiate with rating agencies, and find suitable markets for pricing in order to introduce and establish new asset classes in the national or international capital markets. Investors typically provide funds for three tranches according to their individual risk-return profiles and may include both public and private investors.

To close the asset quality or risk gaps between the asset pool and investors' requirements a guarantor or credit enhancer may be necessary in order to introduce new asset classes into emerging markets. Beyond the development of new asset classes, the credit enhancer aims to create sustainable capital market development. The eventual goal is for the originator to access funds without third-party credit enhancement.

Major Stakeholders

Donors include bilateral and multilateral aid agencies that provide official development cooperation assistance, and private donors such as foundations and NGOs such as DOEN Foundation and Cordaid. Donors pursue developmental objectives promoting financial sector development, especially in areas such as microfinance, SME, low-cost housing, municipal and environmental finance.

Table 1. Donor profile

Roles	TA provider; investor (in junior tranches); initiating policy dialogue
Risk-Return Profile*	Risk-taker, low risk sensitivity[5]
Motivation and Objectives	Sustainable impact of SF on financial sector development and pro-poor finance
Contributions	Policy dialogue to improve legal and regulatory framework conditions for SF transactions Covering SF up-front and transaction costs TA for MFIs (e.g. governance, transparency, management, fiduciary standards, MIS) Preparing 2nd and 3rd "generation" MFIs for SF (capacity building, formalization, promotion of SF standards, ratings) Covering first-loss tranches

* *simplified categorisation*

[5] The risk-return profile is not static. It has to be considered as a flexible relationship. The low risk sensitivity of donors does not mean that they are willing to accept any kind of risk independently of the expected developmental returns.

Donors play a vital role in preparing the ground for successful SF transactions in emerging market countries, mainly through three instruments: They provide technical assistance (TA) to promote and upgrade banks and to cover the up-front costs of SF transactions; they initiate a policy dialogue with governments in order to improve legal and regulatory practices and frameworks for SF transactions; and they cover the most risky part of SF transactions.

Development Finance Institutions (DFIs) and International Financial Institutions (IFIs)[6]

DFIs are development agencies or banks such as KfW, FMO and DEG, some of which are governed under the Basel supervisory regime. They act under similar rules, regulations and limitations as commercial banks. IFIs include e.g. ADB, IFC and EBRD and have fewer limitations which in principle allow them to take higher risks compared to DFIs.

DFIs like KfW play a dual role in development finance: KfW Development Bank acts as agent for the German government using grants for TA and concessional loans from the federal budget and guarantees covered by the Government. In addition, KfW provides loans from its own resources at market rates in complementing limited subsidized funds classified as official development assistance (ODA).

As financial institutions with development expertise, DFIs have "the best of both worlds": detailed knowledge of the financial sectors in emerging market countries and its legal and regulatory environment on the one hand, and standing as triple-A-rated institutions in the commercial world on the other. For example, DFIs have been instrumental in supporting microfinance through TA, loans and equity, using institutional strategies like greenfielding, down-scaling or upgrading. In addition, KfW, for example, has also gained a vast experience with SF transactions in Germany and elsewhere in Europe.

DFIs can perform the following functions in SF transactions: 1) they take an active role in structuring risks as the lead or structuring investor by becoming involved in the SF transaction at its inception; 2) due to their developmental orientation, they can take higher risks compared to commercial investors, taking the mezzanine tranches, while offering senior tranches to more risk sensitive investors; and 3) they can provide various credit enhancement instruments such as guarantees to achieve essential triple-A-ratings. DFIs are well positioned to act as "honest brokers" with regulators to overcome legal and/or regulatory hurdles, permitting the introduction of SF to a new market or asset class in emerging market countries.

---

6 For the sake of simplicity DFIs and IFIs are referred to as DFIs, ignoring the differences noted.

DFIs facilitate the establishment of microfinance, SME finance, low-cost housing and environmental finance as well-defined asset classes. They assume this role by active involvement in deal structuring, credit enhancement and as investor in subordinated tranches, signaling to commercial investors the credibility of the SF transaction. In that sense DFIs provide significant quality enhancements and necessary comfort for private capital even in the absence of international recognized ratings. In addition, SF transactions are considered as pivotal instruments to develop local capital markets.

Table 2. DFI profile

Roles	Lead, structuring and anchor investor; credit-enhancer (guarantor); investor (mostly in mezzanine and senior tranches); dialogue with regulators
Risk-Return Profile*	Medium risk appetite[7]
Motivation and Objectives	Sustainable impact of SF on financial sector development and pro-poor finance combined with reasonable return on investment
Contributions	Risk mitigation by providing guarantees Co-investors in junior notes/subordinated tranches Investment of own funds in senior tranches to signal credibility of SF deals Knowledge of both development finance and private capital markets Covering SF up-front and transaction costs Conducting due diligence on originator and asset pool Preventing mission drift in structured funds Facilitating local currency financing (hedging foreign exchange risk) Providing temporary replacements for international ratings of newly introduced asset classes Facilitating establishment of micro-finance, SME finance, low-cost housing and environmental finance as well-defined commercial asset classes

* *simplified categorisation*

[7] The risk appetite of DFIs should generally be higher than the risk-return profiles of donors and lower than those of private investors. This does not negate the logic of transactions where private investors take more risks than DFIs by investing in the first loss tranche, because they consider the risk acceptable in relation to the expected return. See the db Microfinance-Invest Nr. 1 deal.

Private Investors

Two types of investors can be identified: *commercial investors and the socially motivated or dual-objective investors.* Commercial investors include a vast variety of actors such as institutional investors, pension funds and insurance companies, investment banks, hedge funds, oil and state funds, as well as high net worth individuals who may also be dual-objective investors.

Commercial investors' decisions are guided by asset allocation strategies that define the range of possible investments and the proportion of each asset class they will buy for a given portfolio, weighing risk and return with the objective of obtaining the highest possible return. Commercial investors compare different investment options based on the respective risk-return potentials. Benchmarks and ratings provided by international rating agencies for different risk classes are major tools used to determine the comparability of various investment alternatives.

Banks that are unrated and the absence of international ratings and benchmarks, combined with insufficient information and the lack of confidence of commercial investors unfamiliar with a new asset class makes this relationship a bit precarious. The risk and return profile of commercial investments are normally compared to an established asset class benchmark (i.e. Standard & Poor's 500). Because loans to banks or portfolios of loans to SMEs and low-income households in emerging market countries are not yet a well-defined asset class, investments in these banks do not fit into the analytical framework governing commercial investor asset allocation. Benchmarking could be achieved by ratings from international rating agencies, but to date only national ratings for a few banks have been awarded. Moreover, even international ratings would be restricted by the sovereign ceiling of the respective country rating. As a consequence, structured development finance transactions in emerging markets would find it difficult to receive a rating from international rating agencies acceptable to commercial investors.

Commercial investors can provide very large funds compared to public development funds. Commercial investors will therefore have to provide most of the investment for the expansion of banks in emerging market countries. Therefore, mainstreaming of development finance cannot be achieved without private capital.

The second group is *socially motivated or dual-objective investors* such as private foundations like the Bill and Melinda Gates Foundation, and responsAbility emphasizing a social return with adequate or marginal financial benefit.[8] While these investors have investment restrictions similar to institutional investors, they also have "a natural predisposition to consider pro-poor-like investments"[9] and do not seek profit maximization.

---

[8] Goodman: Microfinance Investment Funds: Objectives, Players, Potential. In: Matthäus-Maier/Pischke (2006), p. 22.

[9] Sousa-Shields: Commercial Investment in Microfinance: A Class by Itself? In: Matthäus-Maier/Pischke (2006), p. 91.

Table 3. Commercial investor profile

Roles	Arranger and investor (in senior tranches)
Risk-Return Profile*	Highly risk averse; investments in high-grade (triple-A) tradable securities[10]
Motivation and Objectives	Maximum returns
Contributions	Expertise in capital market operations and requirements Coordinate/communicate with rating agencies, commercial investors Can provide very large funds for SF transactions

* *simplified categorisation*

Table 4. Dual-objective investor profile

Roles	Investor (in senior tranches)
Risk-Return Profile*	Highly risk averse[11]
Motivation and Objectives	Adequate financial return combined with reputational, "social" or environmental return
Contributions	Can provide very large funds for SF transactions

* *simplified categorisation*

Roles, Contributions and Interplay of Various Stakeholders

In development finance, true sale securitisation such as asset backed securities (ABS) and collateralised debt obligations (CDO) together with structured investment funds have played a major role in SF.[12] A common feature of all these transactions is the involvement of public sector stakeholders as donors and/or as DFIs.

The role of donors and DFIs depends on the stage of SF and on the contributions of private capital and public actors. In the initial phase of establishing new asset classes or markets, donors and DFIs are strategically important in creating

[10] The high risk aversion of private investors is a simplified generalisation. Cases like the db Microfinance-Invest Nr. 1 deal, where the private investor takes more risks than the DFI, should be seen as the result of a changed perception of risk by the private investor, not as lower risk aversion.

[11] See footnote 6.

[12] Glaubitt, Hagen, Feist, Beck: Reducing Barriers to Microfinance Funding: The Role of Structured Finance, p. 9.

and testing SF. Donors and DFIs are prepared to accept a higher level of risk, while private capital is almost always risk-sensitive as illustrated in Figure 8. DFIs have a different risk perception through their better knowledge of MFIs and their difficult markets and environments, while commercial investors are less familiar with banks and their environment, thus overestimating risks. The function of public stakeholders is to match (perceived) investment risk with the risk tolerance or appetite of commercial investors. This can be generally accomplished by constructing hierarchical divisions or "risk-ladders" bearing different types of risks and corresponding returns.

Depending on clients, markets and structures, donors and DFIs can play different roles in initiating and complementing commercial investors. Donors can provide public grant funding for first loss cushions, taking the highest risk portion based on developmental objectives. Donors and DFIs provide TA to support banks in meeting the high governance, transparency and reporting standards of international capital markets and investors. In addition, donors can offer TA or other grants to cover the up-front cost of establishing SF vehicles, and DFIs and IFIs use their resources and personnel to bear administrative costs. There is a wide consensus that public investors are usually the first movers and invest where private investors are not able or willing. When an asset class is eventually established, donors and DFIs can focus on new classes.

DFIs like IFC, EBRD or KfW can act as *structuring/lead or anchor investor*, actively designing or structuring the deal from the beginning and assisting the originator and arranger. As structuring investor, DFIs do not only take risk in the deals in which they participate, but also mitigate risks.[13] This is done, for example, by bringing in legal expertise, by conducting thorough due-diligence on the originator and the asset pool, and by monitoring the transaction and initiating discussions with rating agencies and other counterparties.

In addition, banks involved in securitisation transactions for the first time very often need advice. In these cases, DFIs can play the role of an *honest broker,* because they are trusted by the banks. In addition, DFIs are not considered potential competitors. Finally, they have the expertise and TA-capacities to support banks on legal and regulatory issues.

In the *BRAC Micro Credit Securitisation,* the first on-shore securitisation of a microloan portfolio, KfW provided substantial technical advice to the arranger, RSA Capital, and actively lobbied for the deal with Bangladeshi authorities.[14] The legal and regulatory environment in emerging market countries often inhibits the development of local capital markets – especially securitisation transactions. In such circumstances, donors and DFIs such as KfW have the clout to initiate policy dialogue with government and regulatory and supervisory agencies that can make

---

[13] Lee Meddin: Foreword – Establishing new markets for securitisation: The value-added of the credit enhancer.

[14] For more details see Hüttenrauch and Schneider, p. 42 (to be changed in galley proof).

SF development possible. In addition, they can finance legal and regulatory feasibility studies. These activities are especially important for initial SF transactions in a market in which private investors would be unwilling to deal.

In addition to several risk mitigating features, the Credit Agency of Bangladesh rated this first local asset based securitization (ABS) issue AAA in a local rating. The Dutch development bank, FMO, purchased one-third of the securities. Citibank Bangladesh and two other local commercial banks also took one-third. Citibank Bangladesh purchased the remaining third, backed by a guarantee from FMO and a counter guarantee from KfW covering timely payment of interest and principal.

In the BRAC securitisation, FMO and KfW did not only provide necessary *credit-enhancement*. KfW acted as structuring investor and provided substantial input in the design of the final structure of the deal. FMO's investment in one-third of the securities signaled its confidence and trust in this new asset class, acting as a catalyst for commercial investors.

Microfinance Loan Obligations 1 (MFLO 1) – Opportunity Eastern Europe Securitisation was a similar transaction. The European Investment Fund (EIF) played a complementary role in the deal structure, acting as co-arranger and guarantor of the timely payment of interest and principal for the senior notes. As the originating banks had never been rated by an internationally recognised rating agency, KfW calculated the average rating of the total pool as B+ at closing. Given the subordination structure and first loss tranche, the senior notes would have been assigned a BB rating. Through the guarantee of the EIF and its AAA rating, the guaranteed senior notes were assigned a triple-A-rating. In addition, KfW invested almost EUR 20 million in senior notes, providing confidence to commercial investors. Similar credit enhancements have been provided by DFIs in other microfinance deals. *BlueOrchard Microfinance Securities I* was the first securitisation of microfinance assets.[15] The US government's Overseas Private Investment Corporation (OPIC), a development finance institution, issued fully guaranteed certificates of participation to institutional and private investors (senior note holders), guaranteeing their investments and supporting the credibility of the transaction.[16] JP Morgan Securities distributed the securities to institutional and private investors.[17]

In a subsequent transaction, *BlueOrchard Loans for Development 2006 ("BlueOrchard II")*, the senior notes were not enhanced with a guarantee by a DFI. Commercial investors were better informed about the MFI asset class, making pure subordination via a waterfall payment structure sufficient.

---

15 Details see Goodman, Microfinance Investment Funds: Objectives, Players, Potential. In: Matthäus-Maier/Pischke (2006), p 25, and Hüttenrauch and Schneider.

16 For more details see Glaubitt, Hagen, Feist, Beck.

17 Brugger: Microfinance Investment Funds: Looking Ahead. In: Matthäus-Maier/Pischke (2006), p. 241.

Securitisation of ProCredit Bank (Bulgaria) was led by Deutsche Bank as arranger in 2006. The partial securitisation of ProCredit Bank's loan portfolio (micro, small and medium enterprise loans) was the first true sale securitisation in Bulgaria. The transaction was facilitated by credit enhancement provided pari passu by KfW and the EIF. By guaranteeing principal and interest payments for the senior notes, the rating of the pool was raised from BBB to AAA, qualifying for Deutsche Bank's asset backed commercial paper program. The guaranteed senior tranche was sold to commercial investors.

These deals demonstrate the role of DFIs as providing *substitutes for international ratings*. The absence of international ratings and benchmarks for the originator's asset quality creates information asymmetries between originator and private investors, which translates into a lack of investor confidence. Therefore, DFIs provide significant quality enhancements and necessary comfort for private capital even in the absence of international recognized ratings for MFIs or SME banks. This is achieved by acting as structuring or lead investor, through credit enhancement in the form of guarantees and by investing their own funds. With their own triple-A-ratings awarded by reputable international rating agencies, DFIs are the perfect interim substitute for international ratings.

Private investors view the comparatively high start-up cost of structured finance vehicles as a significant barrier to market entry. This lack of confidence could threaten a transaction. DFIs are generally prepared to assign a significant amount of time, manpower and financial resources to establish structured finance facilities, preparing the ground for private capital.

Furthermore, donors and DFIs are instrumental in increasing the demand for SF by developing and graduating second and third tier banks in emerging market countries.

An interesting example of changes of roles and the contributions of public and private stakeholders is the *db Microfinance-Invest Nr. 1* deal, which closed in July 2007. The deal has innovative features:

- Deutsche Bank took the entire unrated junior tranche for the first time;
- Private commercial investors invested in the mezzanine tranche;
- Private (ultra high net worth) individuals made investments for the first time;
- Subordinated loans to MFIs were securitized for the first time.

KfW co-initiated the deal with Deutsche Bank, and acted as structuring and lead investor in the mezzanine and senior tranches, signaling to private investors their confidence in the deal. Further enhancements were not necessary to attract private investors.

A simplified summary of the different roles and contributions of the various SF stakeholders is shown in figure 2.

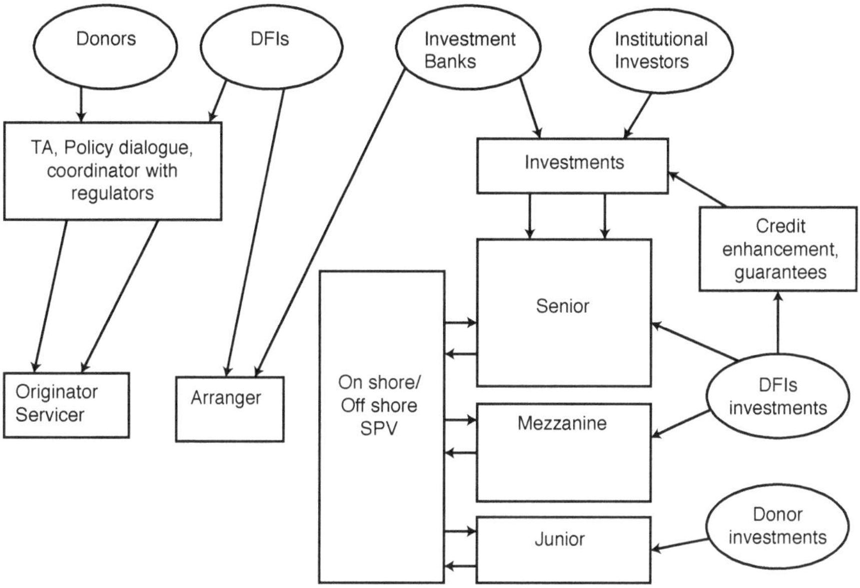

Fig. 2. Roles and contributions of different stakeholders (simplified scheme)

Conclusion

SF seems to be an appropriate vehicle for improving the access of banks in emerging market countries to local and international capital markets. In addition, SF could be very useful in developing local capital markets. To fully develop its potential, SF transactions need donors and DFIs to crowd-in commercial investors. Crowding commercial investors into new asset classes such as MFIs, SMEs or low-cost housing can be accomplished by complementary approaches. These include reducing the preparation and transaction costs of SF, mitigating risks through active deal structuring, shouldering some of the transaction risks through credit enhancement, and generally signaling to commercial investors that microfinance portfolios can be dependable asset classes.

Empirical evidence indicates that commercial investors are not yet ready to invest in SF vehicles without the assistance of DFIs. As SF vehicles for development finance become more mature and commercial investors more confident, donors and DFIs can start to phase out of this asset class and look for new challenges. One promising example is the *db Microfinance-Invest 1* deal which closed in late 2007. This was the first time that Deutsche Bank, a commercial investor, invested in an unrated first loss tranche without additional credit enhancement. At first sight, this deal seems to contradict the simplified categorisations of the risk-return profiles of private investors as presented in this chapter. Deutsche Bank is investing in a higher risk tranche than KfW, but this should be interpreted as a changed perception of risk by the private investor due to better information, not as lower risk aversion. Subsequent SF deals with less or no involvement of DFIs are required to prove that microfinance has successfully been established in international capital markets.

References

Biallas, Margarete; Schwiete, Mark (2006): Investing in Microfinance Investment Funds – Risk Perspectives of a Development Finance Institution. In: Matthäus-Maier, Ingrid; von Pischke, J.D. (eds): Microfinance Investment Funds, Heidelberg, pp. 95.

Brugger, Ernst A. (2006): Microfinance Investment Funds: Looking Ahead. In: Matthäus-Maier, Ingrid; von Pischke, J.D. (eds): Microfinance Investment Funds, Heidelberg, pp. 231.

Byström, Hans (2006): The Microfinance Collateralised Debt Obligation: A Modern Robin Hood? Lund University Sweden.

De Sousa-Shields, Marc (2006): Commercial Investment in Microfinance: A Class by Itself? In: Matthäus-Maier, Ingrid; von Pischke, J.D. (eds): Microfinance Investment Funds, Heidelberg, pp. 81.

Glaubitt, Klaus; Hagen, Hanns Martin; Feist, Johannes; Beck, Monika (2006): Reducing Barriers to Microfinance Funding: The Role of Structured Finance. Paper prepared for the KfW Workshop "Reducing Barriers for Investment in Microfinance: The Role of Structured Finance, Rating and Benchmarking", Frankfurt.

Goodman, Patrick (2006): Microfinance Investment Funds: Objectives, Players, Potential. In: Matthäus-Maier, Ingrid; von Pischke, J.D. (eds): Microfinance Investment Funds, Heidelberg, pp. 11.

Hüttenrauch, Harald; Schneider, Claudia (2005): Securitisation: A Funding Alternative for Microfinance Institutions. Paper prepared for the KfW Financial Sector Conference "New Partnerships for Innovation in Microfinance", Frankfurt.

Jung, Philipp; Erikson, Per-Erik (2006): Microfinance Loan Obligations – Structured Finance for Microfinance Investments. In: Robbe and Ali (eds.) Innovation in Securitisation Yearbook 2006, pp. 179.

Maurer, Klaus (2011): Mobilising Capital for the Poor – How Does Structured Finance Fit in Emerging Markets? In this volume.

Meddin, Lee (2007): Foreword – Establishing New markets for Securitisation: The Value-Added of the Credit-Enhancer. IFC 2007. Website: www.ifc.org/structuredfinance.

Pouliot, Robert (2006): Governance, Transparency, and Accountability in the Microfinance Investment Fund Industry. In: Matthäus-Maier, Ingrid; von Pischke, J.D. (eds): Microfinance Investment Funds, Heidelberg, pp. 147.

CHAPTER 4

Structured Finance – Mobilising New Means to Attract Capital

Ann Rutledge[*]

This article makes the case for structured finance as a viable source of financing for the emerging markets because it is a source of working capital to small and medium-sized enterprises (SMEs) at a cost generally reserved for larger, more capital market worthy firms.

Structured finance extends the range of traditional corporate finance with deeper information on financial and more targeted risk pairing, so that the emerging market borrower is better off and the lender no worse off than in straight corporate debt. In a good scenario, the structuring permits the liquid proceeds of the issuance to be maximized while, at the same time, a reduction in the weighted average cost of capital can be achieved. The difference is the assumption of a lifecycle model of the firm instead of the static *going concern* model that reinforces the *status quo* because it favours businesses with longer histories.

Because the lifecycle model is more sensitive to balance sheet improvement and deterioration, it bolsters investor confidence by providing early signals on improved corporate health and balance sheet deterioration. This sensitivity is bolstered by the ability to use a wide range of financial data including (in the case of securitization) account level data on receivables delinquency, default and recovery. Their short-term time horizon makes it possible to witness the cycle of "birth maturation and death" of the atomized corporation in a more continuous framework. Once this conceptual leap is made, it is but a short step to see, further, that traditional corporate finance only serves mature corporations well (corporations that lie above the dotted line in Figure 1 below) and that to measure the value and risk securities issued by companies in their growing and declining phases (at the wings in Figure 1), more data intensity is required.

Data-intensity makes it possible for the skilled analyst to tease out reasonable projections of free cash flow from operations and project cash flow value from receivables static pool history. Risk pairing and capital efficiency are also improved because the capital structure of the debt offering can be partitioned more precisely to cater to the widest number of interested investors. By contrast, traditional

* Founding Principal, R&R Consulting.

corporate finance methods used to monitor the health of large firms in the developed world do a generally poor job of distinguishing between small firms that have the franchise strength and staying power to grow into big firms and those that are doomed to failure. All the more so for an SME in the emerging markets.

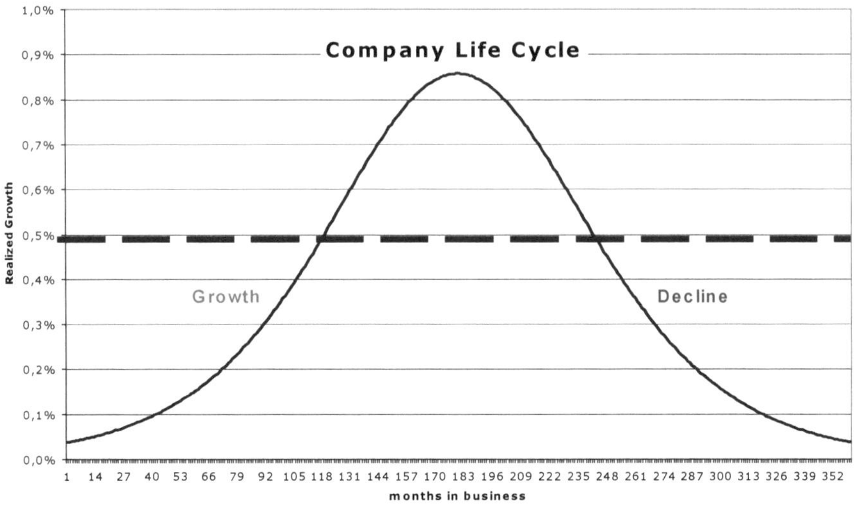

Fig. 1. Life cycle vs. the going concern model

Differences in the culture, the environment and the stage of development impose high barriers to understanding franchise value from a developed market point of departure and perspective.

A key reason why the SME sector is hard to analyze using traditional company finance methods is the reliance on fundamental accounting information, which is stylized and backward looking. An ancillary reason is that, by standard modern financial theoretic methods, value tends to be inferred from secondary market asset prices and not the other way around, even though the decoupling of value from price is a well-known phenomenon, at least on the trading floor. Casting these points in the special language of structured finance, the information arguments underlying asset backed securities (ABS) and mortgage backed securities (MBS) (collectively, securitizations) are more precise because they go farther than accounting information; the analysis of SME historical and current receivables data often leads to the discovery of a corporate rating (pricing) arbitrage whereby the intrinsic value of assets on the balance sheet is higher than the outside lenders perceive. By contrast, the pooling and repackaging of liabilities does not reveal a value discrepancy, but if it stimulates more liquid interest in SME securities or loans, the ancillary benefit of lowering market spreads can also be realized.

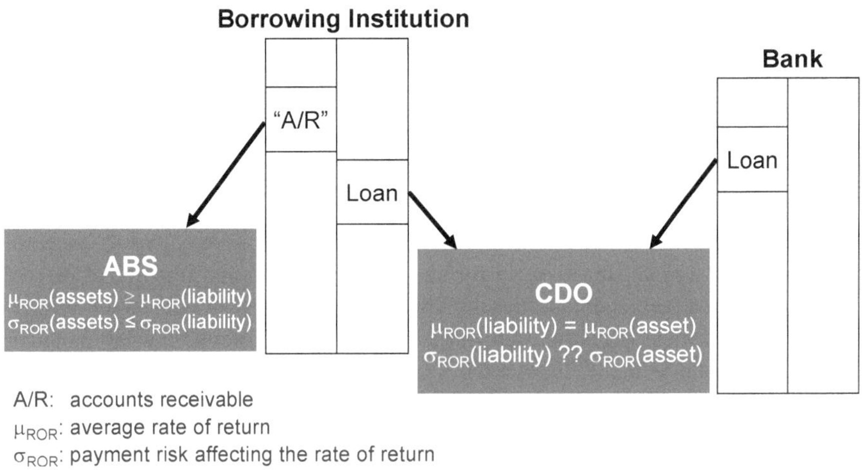

Fig. 2. ABS, Collateralized Debt Obligations (CDOs) and the borrowing institution's balance sheet[1]

Besides these information arguments, another factor favouring structured finance is the plasticity of capital structure. Operating firms are unable to change their innate risk profile over the short- or medium-term. This rigidity curtails the borrower's ability to match investor credit or portfolio risk appetite with the security design. To illustrate, a general obligation of a corporation based in a country where the rating is Non-Investment Grade might be off-limits to investors who could invest in a senior slice of a transaction collateralized by multiple borrowers where the corporation is but one constituent.

Despite the positive rationales offered above, the perception that structured finance is ill suited to funding an SME also has legitimate roots.

Borrower Creditworthiness: An SME borrower is still a borrower, and not every borrower is creditworthy. If creditworthiness is defined as the ability and willingness to make a contractually liable payment, some SME borrowers will fail the first criterion while others will fail the second. Despite the fact that pooling cash flows and issuing liabilities with an undivided interest in the whole offers protection against single borrower liquidity or credit events, and even though structuring augments that protection by enhancing the certainty of outcomes, these measures only address statistical risk. At the boundary between debt and equity, the statistical question becomes a stochastic risk. Someone, somewhere in the capital structure, will experience a payment shortfall. Hence, the capital structure must be equipped with a sufficiently large equity layer to protect the senior investors up to

1 The question marks at the standard deviation of payment risk in Figure 2 reflect the fact that the payment risk on the CDO pool is unknown.

the expected threshold of borrower payment risk (reflected in a *rating*) for which they demands market compensation (*risk premium*). The decision where to draw the boundary between debt and equity is based on a thorough analysis of the sources and uses of capital inside the transaction.

The emerging markets also bring us face to face with non-credit stochastic risks like:

The Rule of Law and the Intention of Law: Structured finance works by reapportioning and transferring risk, so for starters, ownership and transfer of private property must be permissible under the law. Securitization, the conversion of contracts into securities, is restricted to jurisdictions where commercial law is sufficiently developed to make the outcomes of sales and pledges of collateral highly predictable. Moreover, since a key goal of securitization is to reduce cost of funds through bankruptcy avoidance, bankruptcy should be an orderly and predictable process in the originator's jurisdiction. If not, an unambiguous method of achieving bankruptcy remoteness must exist. Finally, it is helpful to have banking and security laws that police data disclosure.

Inconsistency or incompleteness in the law introduces a layer of additional risk that does not, in itself, prevent transactions from being structured or sold. Very few jurisdictions provide the perfect legal environment for these deals; more often, certain types of transactions are facilitated but not others. Some legal cultures allow for rather more metaphysics in the commercial law, and future flow transactions (the sale of receivables that do not yet exist) may take place there. Future flow deals are difficult to do in markets where the law does not recognize floating charges. In some countries there is a deep political reluctance to make mortgagors homeless; mortgage securitization is difficult in these environments because uncertainty in the foreclosure process makes an important part of the cash flow (recoveries) hard to value. The United States believes in giving second chances to bankrupt companies, and this philosophy creates a lack of transparency around the bankruptcy process – but still the market has managed to grow. From a market development perspective, the readiness issue has less to do with whether the law is incomplete, and more to do with whether ambiguities in the law are an inducement to openly pilfer another person's promised cash flow.

The Payment System: Since "possession is nine-tenths of the law," the cash belonging to a structured transaction should pass through a structure of accounts belonging exclusively to the investors; but cash flow isolation is not uniformly achievable everywhere. Some jurisdictions have a rudimentary payment system, where it is characteristic for individuals to move the payment on bicycle or on foot from the borrower to a local bank account, where it then makes its way to a designated account that may or may not achieve legal separation from the original lender. In other jurisdictions where payment system infrastructure is ahead of the West, borrowers may be able to pay their mortgages into direct debit accounts. This makes calculating cash positions easier than when payment goes by check into a lock box account but it also imposes an overnight commingling risk. Such imperfections from a pure securitization standpoint do not usually derail transactions. They simply impose a higher cost of capital in the form of extra credit enhancement.

Transaction Intent: Up front, structured finance imposes, new costs on the originator: rating, legal, accounting and trustee fees, and IT expenses are required to support reporting. I believe (and doubt that I am alone in this belief) that some structured deals are created only to generate fees. This comment is especially relevant to the era prior to the Credit Crisis of 2008, when heavy front fee loads were a standard operating procedure. Let this not be true of deals from the markets with the greatest scarcity. The time it takes to study and evaluate the benefits of doing a structured financing imposes opportunity costs. To a great extent, such costs pose a chicken-and-egg problem for originators and investors since the wisdom of these commitments remains uncertain until after the fact. (Often the value of them is borne out – but surprises occur: I once rated a transaction in a new market where the cash flow receipts due to the investors under the indenture were collected but never forwarded to the trust accounts. After some time, both parties agreed to nullify the transaction and the seller repaid the investor.) Understanding the total context – the meaning of the collateral data and the motivation of the transaction structure – is necessary in valuing deals everywhere. For transactions in developing markets, the failure to localize the diligence process defeats the originators' rationale for paying developed world fees to enter this game—to minimize the pricing and liquidity impacts of the profound information asymmetries between the two markets.

Borrower Readiness to Accept Responsibility: Beyond borrower creditworthiness, there is the further question of borrower readiness to perform as required. Before we can further elaborate this point, however, we must first raise a cardinal question overlooked in the *Borrower Creditworthiness* section.

Who Is the Real Borrower? The answer is embedded in the transaction type. For a CDO, it is the microfinance institution (MFI) that lends to micro, small and medium enterprises (MSME) borrowers. For an ABS or real mortgage backed securities (RMBS), the value and risk analysis underlying the transaction traces the cash flow trail back to the micro enterprise. To-date, all structured transactions have repackaged MFI loans in a CDO format. The main reason is due to market development and readiness issues. For, in truth, the readiness analysis is both broad and deep. It addresses aspects that a micro enterprise may not be equipped to answer, for example:

- The integrity of data collected and used by the borrower;
- The existence of systems to collect data, control capital and report results;

- The experiential depth of the credit-granting function;
- The robustness of non-credit risk management systems;
- The diversity of funding alternatives already in place;
- The adequacy of basic operational and administrative infrastructure;
- The alignment of financial incentives with purpose, mission, strategy and tactics; and
- The character, integrity, commitment and vision of company leadership.

But un-readiness (a measure of progress) should never be confused with inertia (a refusal to progress). The securitization readiness exercise will never be fulfilled in one go. Even for the issuing MFI, it needs iteration. Incremental exposure to the thinking process behind the readiness exercise has heuristic value that may take root inside the micro enterprises in various states of un-readiness, as well as to the issuing MFI.

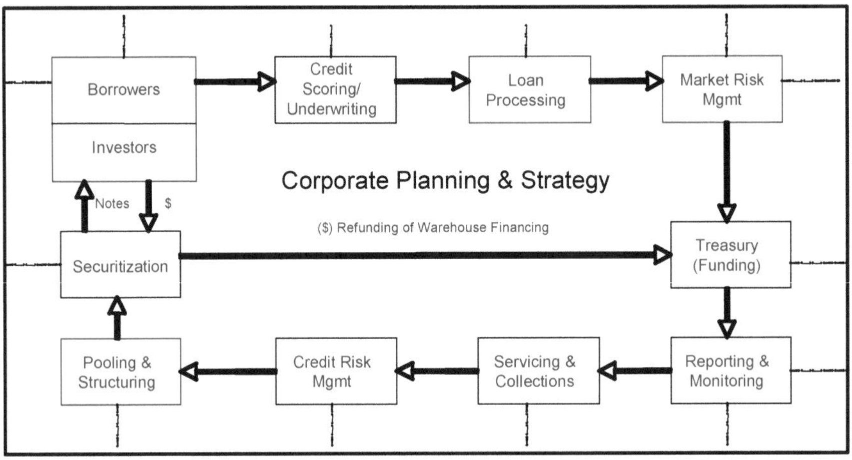

Fig. 3. Securitization readiness – a loop of interlocking relationships

Investor Readiness: Borrower readiness for structured finance is not enough. Investors who claim to support certain economic or financial sector development goals should be prepared to spend the time required to understanding the value proposition being offered in the form of emerging market structured securities. They should know enough about the structuring and pricing process to calculate a fair rate of return for the risk they are taking. Finally—a subtle point—they should be willing psychologically to allow the borrower to prosper and flourish by the ability to borrow at a fair cost of capital.

Market Responsibility Readiness: Structured finance is itself, an emerging financial technique. In the global credit crisis of 2008–2010, it proved to be the conduit for a lot of unwanted leverage and unexpectedly risky assets backed by seemingly safe mortgage paper. We need to recognize that because micro-, small and medium-sized enterprise loan receivables are subject to fewer regulatory and disclosure requirements than commercial or consumer loans from developed markets, financial arrangers seeking to manipulate the loopholes of the structured finance machine may be perversely attracted to them. Hence, it is essential that the process elements of transaction structuring (due diligence, underwriting and capital structure design) be carried out to a very high standard of transparency and openness, to prevent the victimization of parties on both sides of the trade—the borrowers, and the investors. Until a common set of disclosure and underwriting standards becomes accepted and is adopted by the market at large, this precondition is indeed hard to ensure.

Appendix

A Working Glossary of Securitization Terminology

The quest for marginal economic efficiency defines structured finance. It arose out of the ashes of the U.S. Savings & Loan Crisis thirty years ago as a way to extract the value of performing assets locked up in the balance sheets of insolvent institutions. Since then, the structured market has developed wherever repackaging and refinancing assets off-balance sheet has been able to produce marginal economic benefits. Some transaction types are crafted to reduce tax expense; others to lower the corporate cost of funds or required regulatory capital reserves, or to improve liquidity or expand the investor base—as, for example, securities collateralized by microfinance loans exemplify. Besides having different financial objectives, structured transactions also vary widely by asset type, including short and long-dated, large and small ticket, interest- and non-interest-bearing, consumer or commercial, private market contract or public market security. Finally, structured securities vary by "issuer" type: off-balance sheet vehicles of different design elements, which appear to have evolved over time by "natural selection."

The restless, omnivorous path of the structured market's development is reflected in its lexicon, which consists mainly of abbreviations, strings of alphabetic code, like "CDO," "CLO," "CBO," "RMBS," "CMBS," "ABS," "ABCP," and "SIV," that hint at family resemblances but also hide the deep structure of transaction "DNA". To grasp their financial essence it is necessary to develop an intuition for the grammar that binds the economic elements into meaningful units.

As surely as the human sentence has a subject, an object and a verb, all structured transactions are broadly defined in three dimensions: (1) market basis, which refers to the economic purpose of the transaction; (2) market sector, which refers to the institutional role of the borrower; and (3) modelling conventions, which actually follow the market sector—by custom but not necessity.

Market Basis – Purpose of the Transaction

Given that all structured deals redistribute the risk and return characteristics of the collateral being repackaged, the economic purpose (or, in the jargon of structured finance, **market basis**) can be characterized in one of two ways: the purpose of the *cash* or *spot market* is to raise funds more efficiently; the purpose of the *credit derivatives market* is to transfer risk to parties with an appetite to manage it. This distinction dominates the other two dimensions.

Typical cash market mechanics entail a back-to-back sale of collateral to a limited purpose entity (**SPE**, *Special Purpose Entity*, also *SPV*, "v" for vehicle). This separates the collateral's intrinsic default and recovery risk legally (via *true sale*) from the borrower's own, enabling the potential of portfolio diversification to be more fully realized so that the SPE can be justifiably embedded in a more highly levered capital structure. This process underlies all securities with names like strings of alphabetic code. But the on/off balance sheet ritual is an artifact of the bankruptcy code where the transaction takes place. It is utterly inessential in every market but the United States, where bankruptcy necessarily entails reorganization. What is essential is that the pool credit risk be directly re-measured at the point of repackaging, to justify the additional leverage. In that sense, the leveraged buyout — another type of transaction that goes by a name like a string of alphabetic code (*LBO*) — belongs to this category, along with ABS, RMBS, CMBS, CDO, CLO, CBO, ABCP and SIV.

As mentioned above, synthetic credit markets are for risk transfer, not funding. Characteristically, one swap counterparty (the *short*) buys protection against the net default risk (*default, net of recovery*) of reference collateral on its balance sheet by entering into a *credit default swap (CDS*) with the other swap counterparty, which takes the *long* side of the risk trade and receives a swap (insurance-like) premium. (Risk transfer also can take place in a *total return swap*, whereby the long takes default and interest rate risk are neutralized, however this transaction replicates a transfer of ownership, not merely risk, because the entire payment stream is swapped out.) The reference collateral for credit synthetics is determined flexibly and consensually between buyer and seller. It may relate to a corporate debt instrument; an ABS or CDO tranche on the balance sheet of a bank; a financial index with or without a physical collateral; or other intangibles. The risk is similarly customizable. It need not refer to traditional credit risks of the cash market. However, customization comes at the expense of liquidity. Synthetic instruments that mimic the risk of single entities are called *credit default swaps* whereas those that mimic the risk of securitizations, with pooled reference obligations at a target risk level of a capital structure, are called *synthetic collateralized debt obligations* (also, confusingly, CDO).

Market Sector – Institutional Role of the Borrower

Already in the discussion of the previous section, **Market Sector** distinctions have arisen that demand clarification. Market sector defines the features of the issuing vehicle that impart a particular risk contour and disposition to its securities. Three sectors predominate: the "*" Backed Securities, the Collateralized "*" Obligation family, and the Conduit family. For the first case, *Asset/Mortgage Backed Securities* (**ABS/RMBS**) are backed by bundled homogeneous, small-ticket, interest-bearing loan exposures, usually on a strictly non-recourse basis; when recourse is part of the package, it is either a European structure like a covered bond, or it is a structural mistake. Vehicles of this type rarely replenish the collateral base with new collateral ("revolve"); mostly their liabilities amortize in tandem with the assets. The speed and order in which the liabilities amortize are determinants of value, alongside the risk and payment characteristics of the underlying pool. The process of transforming non-public consumer collateral into securities is known as "securitization."

CLO/CBO/CDOs refer to both issuing vehicles and securities fashioned by re-packaging *loans*, *bonds* or, more generally *debt* residing on a bank's balance sheets. Strictly speaking, it is not securitization because the collateral is typically traded already in the capital markets. For cash market CDOs etc., collateral purchases are financed through the issuance of new securities, in an appropriate quantity and structure of leverage given the pool's underlying cash flow or market value. For synthetic CDOs, securities are not issued unless the investor seeks a funded instrument. In the latter case, funding from the issuance of new securities is used to purchase unrelated, generally highly rated collateral as the source of interest and principal payments, while the swap premium is approximately the same as the risk premium on a credit of comparable rating and average life.

CDOs tend to have a limited revolving period, in contrast to Asset-Backed Commercial Paper (ABCP) Conduits or Programs designed with an unlimited revolving period that can be stopped if triggers are breached, and with maximal flexibility in the type of collateral they can accept. ABCP conduits issue series of short-term, highly rated senior debt used by the bank to finance its receivables off-balance sheet obtain so as to obtain regulatory capital relief. The short-dated paper creates an intrinsically large duration mismatch. It is typically resolved by the conduit sponsor or by a syndicate of banks arranged by the sponsor providing liquidity backup to the performing collateral (*borrowing base*).

Modelling Conventions

Underlying the differences in collateral and structure between these three market sectors are some differences of *risk measurement convention* that can lead to rating inconsistencies. Here are three salient examples:

Collateral Risk Measure: ABS and RMBS security risk is more likely to incorporate the analysis of volatility than CDO or ABCP security risk. That is because ABS and RMBS collateral risk analysis uses historical data, whereas CDO risk assessment is based ratings, a measure of defaults and losses but not volatility. Since volatility is a true measure of risk, risk measurement in CDOs and ABCP is forcibly less rigorous.

Credit Enhancement: Capital used to alter the risk profile of structured securities can take the form of XS (excess spread), Subordination or Over-Collateralization (O/C) and Reserve Funds. When the internal resources of the transaction are not transparent to the market, the use of external Guarantees (swaps, surety bonds, collateral insurance) may be necessary to facilitate the transaction. Triggers, a form of contingent capital, are also commonly used to provide additional comfort to investors, beyond the use of internal or external resources. External credit enhancement and triggers are utilized differently in the three market sectors. But, what is noteworthy is that reliance on either introduces risks outside the structured finance model: counterparty risk for third-party guarantees or swaps, model risk for triggers.

Credit Structure: There are two main credit structures at work in structured securities: cash flow and market value. With the former, the estimated timing and amount of cash flow receipts primarily determine how the capital structure is fashioned and hence the degree of protection enjoyed by the securities under different scenarios at different points in time. Cash flow credit structures produce the most stable profile of returns overall. Market value credit structures are shaped by the market value of the collateral. They produce a riskier profile of returns, so much that they are routinely discredited and disappear from the market for periods of time. Unfortunately, sooner or later they always seem to find their way back.

CHAPTER 5

Mobilising Structured Finance for Development – Potential Welfare Benefits and Challenges of Securitisations in Large Emerging Markets

Mehdi Mostowfi[*]

Introduction

Despite the turmoil of the global structured finance market that resulted in an unparalleled financial crisis, securitisation markets have continued to be active in a number of emerging markets.[1] For example, in the Indian asset backed securities ("ABS") market, one of the largest emerging securitisation markets, issuance volume dropped by roughly 50% in the fiscal year[2] 2009 compared to the previous record year but returned to the level of FY 2006 in FY 2010 reflecting an annual increase of more than 40%.[3] The Chinese market like many other emerging markets has also seen consistent activity of securitisation volumes even during the most critical phase of the financial crisis. Motivated by these observations, this chapter analyses the welfare benefits and risks of securitisation transactions for the financial systems of emerging markets.

It begins by giving an overview of benefits and risks of securitisations in general as discussed in the academic literature. It then contrasts the critical aspects of securitisations that contributed to the financial crisis in 2007 with characteristics of emerging market securitisations, and scrutinises the reasons why the structured finance markets in developing countries have by and large shown resilience to the global financial crisis. Further, the chapter highlights the welfare benefits of securitisations for different stakeholders in detail: to the financial institutions originating the loan ("originators"); to the group of "end borrowers" consisting of low-

---

* Professor of Finance and Accounting, RheinMain University of Applied Science.

1 This paper focuses on securitisation as the most important type of structured finance transactions. For a definition of the terms structured finance and securitisation see Jobst (2005). For a description of mechanics and different types of securitisations see Fabozzi (2005) chapters 22–25.

2 The Indian fiscal year begins on April 1st and ends on March 31st. FY 2009 began on April 1st, 2008 and ended on March 31st, 2009.

3 See Internet Content Rating Agency (ICRA) Rating (2010) page 3.

income households, small and medium-sized enterprises (SMEs) and microentrepreneurs; to local and international investors and to the financial sector of developing and transition countries in general.

Particular attention is paid to whether securitisations add value compared to traditional refinancing instruments in a qualitative sense that goes beyond higher availability of loans at more favourable terms. Finally, the chapter discusses three challenges for securitisation of SME and microfinance loans, which are in my view the main areas of concern for structured finance transactions in emerging markets: (1) high first loss guarantee requirements of investors and rating agencies, (2) a lack of liquidity in the securitisation market and (3) weaknesses in the legal and institutional framework, particularly in security enforcement, insolvency regimes and accounting treatment.

Benefits and Risks of Securitisations

A number of studies by academics and multinational research and development institutions highlight the benefits of structured finance as an important tool in financial sector development in advanced economies as well as in emerging markets. These sources discuss key underlying elements required for the development of a well-functioning securitisation market.[4] The studies argue that securitisation enables financial institutions to generate more loans than they could otherwise. This is achieved by enhancing the allocation efficiency of financial disintermediation through the creation of a secondary market for loans.

Further, securitisation may reduce the cost of capital by lowering agency and transaction costs, which enhances the operational efficiency of the financial system. Greater availability of loans and cheaper funding for the originator results in a positive developmental impact on end borrowers. For example, low-income households or SMEs, may receive access to finance that may not be available without securitisation. Finally, securitised assets are attractive to investors. They offer higher rates of return than other bonds with similar credit ratings and they can be more closely aligned to investor appetites. Encouraged by these arguments, development finance institutions ("DFIs") have supported the promotion of the securitisation of mortgages, SME loans and microloans[5] in emerging markets.

Critiques of the securitisation process have gained increased prominence with the collapse of the subprime mortgage market in the financial crisis that began around 2008. The potential contribution of securitisations to the credit crisis has been discussed in a number of studies published since 2009.[6] However, the debate

---

[4] See Jobst (2006) and Arner (2002) for an overview of studies describing the benefits of securitisation in emerging markets.

[5] See Institute for Financial Management and Research (IFMR) (2007) chapter 5 for an overview of selected microfinance securitisation and portfolio purchase transactions.

[6] See for example Martin (2009).

Benefits and Risks of Securitisations	
Securitisations help ...	**Securitisations may cause...**
• enhancing allocational efficiency through risk transfer and creation of a secondary market → more lending with longer maturities	• excessive credit creation induced by undisciplined lending → increased risk of default
• reducing transaction and agency costs → cheaper funding for financial institutions and their clients	• lax monitoring → low recovery rates
• building a diversified portfolio and maximising risk adjusted returns for investors	• illusion of liquidity → price instability in a market downturn

Fig. 1. Benefits and risks of securitisations

over whether structured finance can be blamed for increasing systemic risk is not new: it was initiated by Henry Kaufman many years before the current crisis began.[7]

The main systemic risk factors associated with securitisations are excessive credit creation, reduced incentives for originators to monitor loan assets closely, and the enhanced danger from the illusion of liquidity. These problems include marked-to-market or mark-to-model accounting requirements for financial instruments.

The first risk factor mentioned is the result of a potential originate-to-sell moral hazard that is said to be one of the main causes of the subprime crisis.[8] By enabling loan originators to sell off loans, securitisation creates moral hazard because the lenders do not have to bear the adverse consequences of poor underwriting standards – unless originators are kept accountable through appropriate mitigating factors such as a sizeable equity or first loss tranche. The supporters of this argument believe that originate-to-sell tactics created moral hazard that led to declining underwriting standards and lax lending practices. These in

---

[7] See Kaufman (1999) and Murray (2001) for a critical review of Kaufman's arguments (1999).

[8] See Henry/Goldstein (2008), Schwarcz (2008) for a critical discussion of this argument and Keys et al. (2008) who provide empirical evidence that securitisation did reduce the quality of loan screening for subprime loans.

turn were cited as responsible for the vicious cycle of excessive subprime lending that resulted in ballooning property prices which again facilitated more lending until the bubble burst.

In addition to undisciplined lending policy, some argue that securitisations reduce the incentives of financial intermediaries to carefully monitor their loans and initiate appropriate work-out measures in case of a default.[9]

The illusion-of-liquidity argument highlights that although average trading volumes of ABS are quite limited even in developed countries, IFRS and US GAAP require marked-to-market accounting for these instruments. And for similar loan assets on the book of the originator the historical cost method has to be applied.[10] A central problem that arose with the recent crisis was that the market for ABS ceased to function. No market prices were available, other than fire sale prices.[11] As a consequence, the wave of selling in the market downturn was much greater than it would have been if the assets remained on the books of the originators with higher, although unrealistic, valuations.

To the extent that securitisation increases risk, the problem may also lie in a failure to achieve in practice what is assumed in theory, that is, a failure to transfer the risk of default on securitised assets from the originator to the investors in the manner prescribed by accounting and bank regulations. This problem gains relevance in emerging markets. A low level of financial sector development and a lack of market efficiency in general make the transfer of the default risk from the originator to the investor more difficult than in developed countries. Besides the implications for the systemic risks involved with securitisations, a satisfactory solution to this issue is crucial for an assessment of the welfare benefits of securitisation. The benefits in question include those of low-income households, entrepreneurs and financial intermediaries involved. Attention to this distribution is a prerequisite for a fair partitioning of risks and returns between borrowers, originators and investors.

Securitisation Markets in Developing and Advanced Countries

At first glance, it might be surprising that the structured finance markets in developing countries have shown more stability than those in the US and Europe. Taking India as an example of a large and advanced emerging securitisation market and comparing it with the US mortgage backed securities market reveals fundamental differences, not only in size but also in structure.[12] The fact that the Indian securitisation market experienced only a few downgrades and no losses on investor payouts through early 2009 can be attributed to these differences.

---

9 See Schwarcz (2008) page 9.

10 See Murray (2001) pages 63–64.

11 See Martin (2009) page 14.

12 See CRISIL Rating (2008).

	India	US
Exposure to Mortgage Debt	■ Mortgage Debt Outstanding/GDP approx. 7% ■ MBS/GDP < 1%	■ Mortgage Debt Outstanding/GDP > 80% ■ MBS/GDP approx. 50%
Asset Quality and Credit Enhancement	■ Loan-to-value ratios below 80% ■ First loss ratios: 5% - 25%	■ Loan-to-value ratios exceeding 100% ■ First loss ratios: 1% - 4%
Originate-to-Sell Model	■ Far less than 10% of mortgage loans are securitised	■ More than 60% of mortgage loans are securitised
Complexity of Securitised Loans and MBS-Structures	■ Fixed-rate loans dominate ■ Regulatory restricitions on synthethic securitisation, so MBS market is characterised by simple structures and products	■ Large proportion of floating-rate- and interest-only loans ■ Presence of highly complex MBS structures and products

Fig. 2. Comparison of key parameters of Indian and the US markets
Data source: Credit Rating Information Series of India (CRISIL) Rating (2008).

As a result of risk adverse prudent underwriting policies, Indian banks have been slow to offer mortgage loans to their customers.[13] And so far regulators and banks have not allowed subprime mortgage lending in India.[14] Mortgage lending is usually made on conservative terms with moderate loan-to-value ratios to middle and upper income households. This implies that India, like most emerging markets, is far from being at risk of imprudent credit generation. For some time to come, emerging markets will continue to suffer from risk adverse behaviour through lack of capital and insufficient credit generation.

Further, transaction structures with high first loss ratios as required by rating agencies and investors give a strong incentive to the originating financial institutions to pursue a conservative and disciplined lending policy, both for "originate-to-sell" loans as well as for those they intend to keep on their own books.

Another often cited reason for the subprime crisis in the US is the complexity of the terms of certain mortgage loan agreements on the one hand and the complexity of the MBS structures and products on the other hand. Subprime mortgage loans in the US were increasingly made with "innovative" terms, such as adjustable interest rates, interest-only payment options and negative amortisation so that some borrowers failed to understand the risks they incurred.[15] Further, complex

---

[13] This also applies to consumer loans, SME and microloans.

[14] Broadly speaking this also applies to other emerging markets, see Gwinner/Sanders (2008), p. 30.

[15] See Schwarcz (2008) page 11.

MBS structures, particularly those with synthetic elements, overwhelmed even the expertise of professional investors who used complex mathematical models that they apparently did not fully understand.

In contrast to the US, the Indian mortgage market is dominated by "plain-vanilla" fixed interest loans. Further, the MBS structures in India, mainly true sales, are quite simple, usually comprising a first loss piece, a second loss piece and a senior tranche. So the terms of the loans, the MBS structures and the potential risks associated with them are highly transparent and easy to understand for end borrowers and MBS investors.

To summarise, prudential policies were instrumental in protecting the Indian structured finance market from a spill-over into the US subprime crisis. This is an important lesson, not only for emerging markets, but also for policymakers and regulators in more advanced countries.[16]

Benefits for Different Stakeholders

Benefits to Originators

Securitisation enables banks to concentrate on origination, servicing and transferring ownership of securitised assets and their risks to capital market investors. In doing so, capital is released for incremental business. The benefits of securitisation for the originators may be:[17]

a) Access to long term funding.

b) Expanding instruments for asset-liability management: the longer maturities of ABS/MBS notes exceed those of corporate bonds in emerging markets, enabling the originator to reduce interest rate and maturity mismatch risks.

c) A mechanism for releasing regulatory capital, if the first loss piece or most junior tranche retained by the originator is less than the regulatory charge for the underlying portfolio that is sold or hedged. The released capital can be re-deployed, effectively leveraging the regulatory capital base.

d) Ability to raise funds in the market based on their asset risk rather than corporate risk. This may imply a lower cost of funds, if the quality and rating of the assets exceed that of the originator's.

e) Better knowledge of the assets, which leads to improved credit risk management, operating efficiency, as well as product and customer focus ("capacity building effect on financial institutions").

---

[16] See Gwinner/Sanders (2008) for a detailed discussion of the lessons from the subprime crisis and the implications for emerging markets.

[17] See also GBRW (2004) page 29.

f) Diversification of the investor base and possible positive impact on the reputation of the financial institution.

Benefits to Borrowing Enterprises

Clear benefits for SMEs and other end borrowers may be the following:

a) Higher availability of longer-term funding with manageable repayment instalments for borrowers.

b) Rating analysis and market pricing provide feedback for origination and should improve the management of banks' credit portfolios with greater differentiation of good credits from bad credits. Over time, better performing SME clients may benefit from this market-oriented pricing. Conversely, poorer performing clients would experience a negative impact.

c) The standardisation of products induced by securitisation may lead to a reduction of costs for borrowers, although some borrowers may lose flexibility in terms and conditions.

Benefits to Investors

Investors may enjoy the following benefits:

a) As a new asset class, emerging market ABS/MBS allow investors to construct more diversified portfolios.

b) Emerging market ABS/MBS may offer an attractive investment opportunity for dual-objective (socially responsible) investors.

c) Senior ABS/MBS tranches offer higher returns than equally rated corporate or government debt at higher risk.[18]

d) Subordinated tranches provide an attractive (asset specific) investment opportunity for mezzanine and high yield funds.

Impact on Relationship Between Originator and End borrower

Given that the administration of the loan portfolio (i.e. servicing) remains in the hands of the originator, the day-to-day relationship between originator and end borrower is not affected by the securitisation transaction. The end borrower may not even be aware of it. However, the benefits mentioned above produce a larger volume of loans with better conditions which may have a positive impact on customer loyalty.

---

[18] See Martin (2009) page 8 for an explanation why AAA-rated MBS are traded with a spread over government bonds.

Capital Market and Financial Sector Development

At a macro level the contribution of securitisations to the capital market and financial sector development in emerging markets may include the following impacts:

a) The creation of a secondary market for loan securitisations may catalyse mobilisation of capital from mutual and pension funds that can provide liquidity, even at times when SME/microfinance lenders are cash-strapped.

b) By mobilising funding from foreign investors, securitisations help to connect local capital markets with international capital markets.

c) A liquid market for ABS/MBS instruments may contribute to the development of corporate and municipal bond markets, because infrastructure and the legal framework for trading both instruments are quite similar.

Problems of Securitisations in Emerging Markets

High First Loss Guarantee Requirements

Most SME and microloan securitisation transactions in emerging markets include high first loss guarantees ("FLG") by the originator, ranging from 8 to 20% of the total issuance volume. A substantial part of the guarantee usually has to be covered by cash collateral. At the same time, the default rate of SME loans and microloans that are eligible for securitisation transactions is often far below 3%. This implies over-collateralisation of securitised loans at the expense of the originator and the end borrowers, which means that practically no risk transfer takes place between originator and investors.

The main purpose of over-collateralisation is to mitigate the "originate-to-sell" moral hazard problem described above: The higher the FLG, the greater the incentive the originator has to pursue a disciplined and conservative lending policy, which requires securitising only high quality assets and monitoring loan performance properly. However, high over-collateralisation also limits the benefits of securitisations to originators and end borrowers. First, high FLG reduce the potential for regulatory capital relief, reduce the pace of loan portfolio growth (without external equity injections) and lower the return on equity to the originating financial institution.[19] Further, higher equity requirements for securitised assets imply an increased cost of the loan for the end borrower, because the originator prices the loan at a level that covers the cost of equity.

The high levels of FLG can mainly be attributed to the high risk aversion in the market. The agencies defend their risk aversion as being a result of two factors:

---

[19] Note that the Basel II framework as well as national guidelines for securitisation in most emerging markets require full deduction of first-loss-guarantees from tier-one capital.

(1) the originators' absence of a track record and (2) their own limited familiarity with this asset class. A further reason for the high FLG is that in many developing countries the investor groups buying securitised loans consist mainly of a small number of large commercial banks. These banks may be inclined to use their power to force the originators to accept their conditions as long as there is no alternative refinancing.

Rating agencies and large commercial banks investing in securitised loans argue that the FLG requirement will decrease as the originators build a track record of securitised loans and as the level of sophistication of the capital market increases. However, depending on how quickly the FLG levels observed in emerging markets decline to a level that reflects the actual expected default rates, the adverse selection problem noted above contains a significant element of market failure. This issue merits more attention from development finance institutions and regulators.

Lack of Liquidity in the Securitisation Market

In many developing countries, even in those with more advanced capital markets, the securitised loan market is not particularly liquid. A small number of commercial banks and pension and provident funds are the only investors in ABS/MBS.

The illiquidity of securitised loans means that investors have to be prepared to hold the bonds to maturity. This implies that investors require an illiquidity discount which largely offsets the main advantage of securitised loans compared to traditional loans.

This problem can be addressed only by promoting a more liquid market for government and corporate bonds in general. A benchmark yield curve has to be created through the issuance of government bonds and the creation of the infrastructure necessary for trading government and corporate debt. DFIs can play an important role here by acting as market makers for securitised assets or as arrangers of secondary ABS funds. DFIs could also encourage local banks, pension funds and provident funds to provide a market maker platform for securitised assets.

Weaknesses in the Legal and Institutional Framework

Academic research and surveys carried out by DFIs have identified significant weaknesses in the legal frameworks that support securitisations in many emerging market countries. The creation of a functioning system of securitisation involves the following issues:[20] (1) clear property rights to the assets securing the loans, (2) clear rights to transfer property rights, (3) clear rules of security enforcement, (4) a

[20] See Arner (2002) page 517.

clear and predictable system of taxation and (5) appropriate financial regulation and supervision. Furthermore, transparent and consistent accounting rules adopting Basle II recommendations would (1) enable originators to explain these transactions more easily to potential investors in securitised assets, which would improve the originators' negotiating position and (2) limit the systemic risks that may arise from securitisation transactions as the Basel II rules largely reduce the scope for regulatory arbitrage.[21]

Conclusion

Low-income households and SMEs in emerging markets can indeed benefit from structured finance: securitisations are an efficient refinancing tool for financial institutions and helpful in generating more loans in low volume markets. Among the qualitative and quantitative aspects of securitisations, I believe that some of the most significant benefits of structured finance cannot be replicated with traditional credit instruments. This is especially so for the benefits referred to as capacity building effects on local financial institutions and SMEs. In addition to the benefits of securitisation transactions at the levels of different stakeholders, a well-functioning and liquid market for securitised assets has a positive developmental impact on the government and corporate bond markets and on the capital markets of developing countries in general.

Emerging securitisation markets should continue to focus on basic transaction structures and simple, high quality asset types. They should avoid highly complex securitisation products which are likely to increase leverage. This is an important lesson drawn from the recent collapse of the securitisation markets in the US and in Europe.

Further, to enable a vibrant future for securitisation in emerging markets, it is important to ensure a fair partitioning of benefits and risks between borrowers, originators and investors. In this regard, shortcomings such as excessive over-collateralisation requirements and the illiquidity of ABS have to be overcome. DFIs can play a major role in removing these obstacles.

References

Arner, Douglas (2002): "Emerging Market Economies and Government Promotion of Securitisation", 12 Duke Journal of Comparative and International Law, pp. 505–519.

CRISIL Rating (2008): "Indian Securitisation Market Solid Against Global Meltdown", Sector Report December 2008.

[21] Some developing countries have already adopted the Basel II rules. In India, for example, the implementation of Basel II was completed in March 2009.

GBRW (2004): "Study on Asset Backed Securities: Impact and Use of ABS on SME Finance", London.

Gwinner, William; Sanders, Anthony (2008): "The Subprime Crisis: Implications for Emerging Markets", World Bank, Policy Research Working Paper 4726.

Fabozzi, Frank (2005): "The Handbook of Fixed Income Securities", 7th ed., McGraw Hill, New York.

Henry, David; Goldstein, Matthew (2008): "The Bear Flu: How it Spread", Business Week, Jan. 7, 2008.

ICRA Rating (2010): "Update on Indian Structured Finance Market", Sector Report, April 2010.

IFMR India (2007): "Securitisation: information for MFIs", Chennai.

Jobst, Andy (2005): "What is Structured Finance", Securitization Conduit 8, 2005/2006.

Jobst, Andy (2006): "Sovereign Securitisation in Emerging Markets", Journal of Structured Finance 12(3).

Kaufman, Henry (1999): "Protecting Against the Next Financial Crisis", Business Economics, July, pp. 56–64.

Keys, Benjamin;Mukherjee, Tenmoy; Seru, Amit; Vig, Vikrant (2008): "Did Securitization Lead to Lax Screening? Evidence from Subprime Loans", EFA 2008 Athens Meeting Paper, Social Science Research Network.

Martin, John D. (2009): "A Primer on the Role of Securitization in the Credit Market Crisis of 2007". In: Kolb, Robert (ed.): "Lessons from the Financial Crisis, Causes, Consequences and Our Economic Future", Wiley.

Murray, Alan (2001): "Has securitization increased risk to the financial system?", Business Economics, January, pp. 63–67.

Schwarcz, Allan (2008): "The Future of Securitization", Duke Public Law and Legal Theory, Paper No. 223.

CHAPTER 6

Structured Finance for Development – Outlook for New Applications

Andreas A. Jobst[*]

Abstract

The chapter offers a glimpse into the future of structured finance for development based on the evolution of securitisation in emerging markets, using recent experiences in structured microfinance as a showcase. It charts possible terrain to be covered by further innovation in structured development finance regarding conceptual foundations, exogenous and endogenous determinants. In particular, the chapter discusses the current use and future potential of new asset classes, such as Islamic microfinance, renewable energy certificates, emission allowances, tuition fees, and other financial assets and future flows.

Introduction

In its basic principle, securitisation replaces credit finance with capital market-based finance that funds economic activity without the lending and deposit-taking activities of banks.[1] In this way, it transforms bilateral risk sharing between borrowers and lenders into market-based refinancing of asset performance by monetising identifiable cash flows from a diversified pool of present or future asset claims of varying maturity and quality into tradable, interest-bearing debt securities. This process serves to mitigate disparities in the availability and cost of credit in primary lending markets by linking singular credit facilities to the aggregate pricing and valuation discipline of capital markets. Thus, it helps remedy deficiencies in financial markets arising from incomplete capital allocation. Securitisation also facilitates the redistribution of asset risks to investors and broader capi-

---

[*] Economist, International Monetary Fund.

[1] Issuers raise funds via securitisation in order to improve their capital management, reconfigure their balance sheet, and enhance their capacity to originate new assets without increasing their capital base by creating new off-balance sheet securities that do not increase the issuer's level of indebtedness. (This process is known as capital optimisation).

tal markets through transformation and fragmentation of asset exposures aimed at diffusing risk concentrations and installing efficient pricing of illiquid exposures. Since credit risk is customized to the preferences and tolerances of agents, the associated tradability of securitized debt allows the synthetic assembly and dynamic adjustment of asset portfolios via secondary markets at low transaction costs.

The collapse of the securitisation market over the second half of 2007 and the ensuing financial crisis (with spillovers into the real sector), however, have cast serious doubt on the economic proposition of unbundling, transforming, and redistributing credit risk through securitisation. Market ruptures caused by the headlong flight to safety during the initial phase of the crisis seem to recede only slowly, leaving the securitisation market largely depressed as banks dispose of non-core assets and raise capital to de-lever their imploding balance sheets while building new capital buffers. In view of a widespread retrenchment of credit, despite sweeping fiscal intervention in the financial sector and substantial liquidity injections by central banks, both the scale and persistence of the current financial crisis suggest that pervasive securitisation — together with improvident credit origination, inadequate valuation methods, and insufficient regulatory oversight — can perpetuate market disruptions, with potentially adverse consequences for financial stability and economic growth.

This charge begs the question of how securitisation could have contributed to excessive complacency in financial markets and the sharp deterioration of the economic environment. In response to cost pressures and regulatory reforms over the years, rising sophistication in credit risk management has facilitated the rise of structured finance products. An increasing number of financial institutions adopted an "originate-and-distribute" business strategy of loan origination by using securitisation to transfer credit risk from their balance sheets to other banks, insurance companies, hedge funds, and other financial institutions. At the same time, a declining price of risk caused by a shortage of investible assets and abundant global liquidity helped securitisation develop into an alternative funding channel that inflated credit supply to fuel excessive consumer spending and house price appreciation while debilitating the efficacy of monetary policy.

Although real estate-related securitisation on doubtful collateral quality has led to similar macroeconomic effects in emerging market countries, much of the issuance activity there has traditionally focused on trade finance and infrastructure investment, which continue to be areas of growth. After having nearly ground to a halt, securitisation has staged a modest comeback in 2010 and – most remarkably – continues to churn out innovations and grows in sophistication in many emerging market countries.

Given the poorly developed local capital markets in many emerging market countries, securitisation still offers an alternative, more cost-efficient funding and risk management mechanism. Since the end of the 1980s, large, highly-rated exporters and banks in developing economies have successfully sponsored securitisation transactions. By selling hard-currency receivables from abroad through future flow *asset-backed securities* (ABS) they were able to pierce relatively low sovereign ratings, which allowed them to borrow at lower cost than through conventional funding methods (Ketkar and Ratha, 2004–2005).

While the credit crisis has fundamentally altered public perception of securitisation, it has also shifted attention away from arbitrage and speculative transactions to securitisation for capital market development. If used for funding (rather than hedging economic activity), securitisation can in fact expand the existing asset base and remedy the lack of investment possibilities. As a result, the landscape of securitisation in emerging markets has been changing dramatically as more and more emerging market countries begin to recognise that asset securitisation can help overcome the scarcity of high-grade, non-sovereign securities in underdeveloped local capital markets.

Small capital markets lack the absorptive capacity to accommodate large foreign (institutional) investments. In developed countries, high absolute levels of public debt have historically facilitated capital market development. In contrast, much lower sustainable debt/GDP ratios in many emerging market countries with significantly smaller capital accounts prevent public debt issuance from reaching the critical mass to sustain the basic infrastructure of fixed income markets, including trading platforms, valuation services, rating agencies, and financial analysts.

In emerging markets, securitisation remains an effective off-balance sheet funding mechanism for the acquisition or creation of assets, such as infrastructure investments and projects. In addition, external issuers have developed structured finance vehicles to refinance lending to emerging market borrowers and to move emerging market assets into new investment instruments as a way to meet increased investor demand for alternative asset exposures. In particular, the commercialisation of microfinance – by local and external issuers – represents yet another important step in the evolution of structured finance in emerging markets. Despite rising diversity of supply and demand, more financial innovation is needed for progress to continue in this area.

This chapter provides a brief review of the general evolution of emerging market securitisation, especially in the context of microfinance. Based on recent issues in the securitisation of emerging market assets, this chapter explores general determinants of structured finance for development purposes. It concludes by highlighting possibilities for further innovation.

Securitisation for Development

Emerging market securitisation is no longer confined to specialised institutions and has expanded both geographically and in product diversity. Financial innovation no longer seems beholden to traditional asset exposures from hard-currency financial flows of the local private sector, such as commercial banks and export-oriented firms. Increasingly, cash-strapped governments securitise receivables from the privatisation of state-owned enterprises, the sale of public property, or outstanding tax collections by governments. Its reach has grown to include development finance, which focuses on funding productive activity or long-term projects of socio-economic significance. These include affordable housing, infrastructure investments, SME funding at market conditions, microfinance, and efficient resource allocation to improve education, energy efficiency and other aspects of public interest. In particular, governments (and local authorities) in several countries have used securitised issuance to (i) fund critical infrastructure and restructuring projects outside budgetary constraints; and (ii) complete industry deregulation with the help of the private sector.

Others have sponsored securitisation via public sector agencies with the long-term aim of developing local capital markets in areas of public interest in order to fund critical infrastructure investments and curb rising home and consumer finance deficits.[2]

Although application of securitisation for development purposes falls largely in the domain of public sector entities and development institutions, new private initiatives are beginning to complement such government-led efforts. Especially, the commercialisation of microfinance has drawn increased private sector involvement and financial ingenuity. In addition, it has become the proving ground for funding techniques for development assistance. Hence, a closer examination of microfinance securitisation produces important empirical insights and serves as an appropriate platform for the exploration of securitisation to finance development and for discovering areas of financial innovation beyond structured microfinance.

Microfinance Securitisation

Microfinance specialises in the origination of small loans for productive activities and the provision of other financial services (savings, insurance, and funds transfers) to low-income clients who are barred from conventional finance and credit channels for lack of a credit history, collateral, or a steady income. Microfinance complements the range of financial services offered by mainstream banks whose organizational structure and business cannot accommodate the high administrative cost and collection risk relative to projected revenues associated with the origination of unsecured and relatively small credits.

Over the last three decades, microfinance has proliferated from its origins in some of the poorest nations in the world into a global industry. In 2009, the Microfinance Information eXchange (MIXmarket) had 1893 reporting microfinance institutions (MFIs) serving 91.6 million borrowers worldwide. Despite this substantial outreach this represents only a small portion of potential low income customers. Charitable donations, government budgets and international development aid will not be capable of closing this shortfall. Hence, the commercialisation of

2 Most governments, however, have used securitisation primarily as an asset-liability management (ALM) tool to foster more favourable external debt dynamics (i.e., lower debt service relative to current account receipts) and greater fiscal consolidation (i.e., lower public debt relative to GDP) by monetising tax receivables, oil and gas royalties, future water receivables, toll road revenues, and repayments of public sector loans.

microfinance by profit-oriented capital market-based finance is seen as a way to increase supply, diversify funding, and widen the spectrum of services.

MFIs include public sector agencies, dual-objective or social investors, microfinance credit unions, and even private commercial banks. Charitable donations and international development aid are not capable of redressing this shortfall.

Box 1. The Mechanisms and Characteristics of Microfinance

Basic microfinance lending relies on social sanctions and screening through either collective guarantees (*group lending*) or comprehensive borrower background checks paired with progressively larger loan sizes (*individual lending*) in order to overcome credit market inefficiencies from asymmetric information and the limited liability of borrowers without collateral.

In group lending, borrowers receive funds individually but are required to form groups with fellow borrowers who hold joint responsibility for each other's repayment obligations. Depending on the rules governing events of individual default, all members may lose their borrowing privileges. The "joint liability" underlying the group lending concept of microfinance is predicated on peer monitoring. This establishes repayment incentives while limiting both adverse selection and moral hazard from asymmetric information and lowers interest rates – especially if applied to borrowers in small communities with strong family-based ties.

First, group lending induces self-selection of borrowers. Unlike conventional individual lending, which entails the adverse selection of riskier borrowers at higher interest rates, group lending allows micro lenders to avoid some of the agency cost of dealing with risky borrowers by delegating the borrower screening to market-based self-selection. Since safer borrowers would prefer to form lending groups with fellow applicants that share similar riskiness, they face lower repayment cost than risky borrowers, who are on average more likely to bail out defaulting peers. Therefore, in an environment of efficient self-selection, rational expectations about higher borrowing costs deter risky borrowing, which decreases the incidence of default while reducing the effective interest rate.

Second, sharing the cost of default is a disciplining device against moral hazard, while ensuring efficiency gains (due to geographical proximity and trade links) from the effective delegation of monitoring (the effort choice) to group members. Peer monitoring does not require costly verification of borrowers by lenders, and implies more credible and immediate economic and social sanctions when risky projects are chosen. Since project returns are observable to group members ("effort choice"), group lending with joint responsibility lowers the incidence of strategic default or delinquent repayment as borrowers have the incentive to protect their true realization of returns.

Microfinance securitisation conveys the same economic benefits that conventional structured finance purports to generate, such as the active management of a designated asset portfolio, enhanced asset-liability management, and the isolation of certain assets in order to make them self-financing at a fair market rate. There are three basic forms of structured microfinance: (i) microfinance investment funds;[3] (ii) "direct securitisation" (as local issuance), where MFIs commoditise micro lending by issuing standardised securities backed by own microloans; and (iii) "indirect securitisation" (as external issuance) which allows more advanced financial institutions to restructure and securitise debt issued by local MFIs that lack the expertise and sophistication to access international capital markets directly.

Local securitisation for development is limited. Despite the importance of securitization for local capital market development, "direct securitisation" of microfinance receivables is still in its infancy. The premier issuance of this kind was completed in Bangladesh in 2005 by BRAC, formerly known as the Bangladesh Rural Advancement Committee. BRAC is a national private development organisation promoting income generation, social development, healthcare, education, and microfinance for the rural poor in Bangladesh. BRAC disburses microloans through regional and local working groups in which members assess each other's applications for very small short-term loans.

Under the securitization BRAC transferred microloans to a special purpose trust which securitised the repayment proceeds as a five-year series of short-term zero-coupon bonds. In each year of the transaction, the Dutch Development Finance Company (FMO) bought local currency denominated trust debt certificates for a total of USD 8 million and issued a debt guarantee – together with German development bank KfW (Kreditanstalt für Wiederaufbau) – to Citibank Dhaka, the asset manager, which also purchased debt certificates for a total of USD 22 million in local currency (Taka) from the trust. Although the transaction had a maximum tenor of one year, all parties agreed to a rollover mechanism which would establish four additional short-term issues with a total notional value of up to USD 180 million.[4]

However the expansion securitisation for development in emerging markets has so far been primarily realized with external rather than domestic issuers. Small local capital markets in many emerging economies simply tend to lack the critical mass to sponsor "home-grown" issuance. Local securitisation is often rendered inefficient by (i) inadequate market practices, (ii) the lack of uniform transaction structures; and (iii) insufficient transparency of asset quality due to weak rating agencies and a nascent institutional investor base (Jobst, 2006).

---

3 Examples of microfinance investment/debt funds include: "The responAbility Global Microfinance Fund", which was established in November 2003 by a group of Swiss banks, and "The Global Commercial Microfinance Consortium Investment Fund," which was launched in 2005 by Deutsche Bank and a consortium of private and public sector institutions (Byström, 2007).

4 ICICI's purchase of microloans from the Indian SHARE Microfin Ltd. in 2004 is a similar transaction.

The involvement of international investment banks as external sponsors of securitised issuance has become a notable feature of structured microfinance. Since 2005, large investment banks have teamed up with specialised asset managers to fund microfinance institutions (MFIs) as a form of "indirect securitisation." The preferred financing vehicle in this regard has been the now much-maligned collateralised debt obligation (CDO) as a means of funnelling money from global capital markets to the tiny start-ups and would-be entrepreneurs in many of the world's poorest countries.

The extension of the CDO technology (see Box 2) to microfinance is remarkable, not least because it demonstrates that CDOs can successfully transform even very illiquid collateral into tradable securities through a combination of active portfolio management, creative security design, and asset diversification. Although CDOs have lost much of their market-wide appeal on account of their role in distorting actual riskiness of investments and spreading risks far and wide during the U.S. subprime mortgage crisis, they still rank high on the agendas of issuers as an expedient mode of microfinance securitisation that can help sidestep many administrative and legal uncertainties of local issuance. Most of the CDOs referencing emerging market assets have been made for hedging sovereign and corporate credit as well as loans to mid-cap firms and private individuals in emerging market countries.

CDOs on microloans or MFI networks are structured in the same way as traditional synthetic CDOs. The SPV sells credit protection via credit default swaps (CDS) and assumes exposure to the securitized assets without legal ownership before issuing credit-linked notes (CLNs) or some other form of partially or unfunded securities to collateralize portions of potential swap obligations. Investors get paid their coupon at the specified rate, and, in the case of default, their notional investment will get written down to the extent of the loss less any credit enhancement through the notional value of subordinated claims or in some other form.

Box 2. Collateralised Debt Obligations (CDOs) and Their Application in Emerging Markets

Collateralised Debt Obligations (CDOs) have been the fastest growing area of structured finance until the onset of the financial crisis in mid-2007. A CDO is a large-scale securitization transaction that is arranged to unbundle, transform and diversify financial risks from a reference portfolio of one or more credit-sensitive asset classes (and possibly different issuers and/or industry sectors). While standard CDOs use the same off-balance sheet structuring technology as *asset-backed securities* (ABSs) (e.g. securities which are themselves repackaged obligations on mortgages, consumer loans, home equity loans, and credit card receivables), their reference portfolios typically include a wider and more diverse range of assets, such as senior secured bank loans, high-yield bonds and *credit default swaps* (CDSs) – as opposed to more homogenous titles, such as mortgages, home equity loans, and credit card receivables in the case of ABSs.

Most CDOs are not static but are administered like a managed fund of designated assets. Managers of CDOs adjust investment exposure over time to meet a pre-specified risk-return profile and/or achieve a certain degree of diversification in response to changes in risk sensitivity, market sentiment and/or timing preferences. Managers monitor and, if necessary, trade credits within the reference portfolio in order to protect the collateral value from impairment due to a deteriorating credit quality. "Lightly managed" reference portfolios allow for some substitution in the context of a defensive management strategy, while a "fully managed" CDO suggests a more active role of asset managers subject to limits and investment guidelines that are determined by the issuers, rating agencies and different levels of risk tolerance of investors. In particular, managed CDOs may also include ABSs, emerging market bonds or even other CDOs as collateral assets (to produce CDOs of CDOs, also called CDO^2) in so-called "pools of pools" structures.

Three main transaction structures dominate CDO issuance: *cash flow, synthetic* and *market value.* While cash flow CDOs, the most common type of CDOs, are structured to pay off liabilities with the cash generated from interest and principal payments of a static pool of collateral assets, synthetic CDOs sell credit protection to create partially funded and highly-leveraged investment on the performance of designated credit exposures (without actually purchasing the reference assets). *Market value* CDO transactions are structured to support liabilities via the value of collateral assets, mostly as a result of active trading of flexible reference portfolios.

In CDOs that are structured for arbitrage (and, thus, are cash flow-based), asset managers focus on the pool's prospects for appreciation with a view to realizing economic gains from the pricing mismatch between investment returns from reference assets (or credit protection premia on exposures) and lower financing cost of generally higher-rated liabilities in the form of issued CDO securities (Jobst, 2010). In contrast, balance sheet CDOs, which can be either cash or synthetic, remove assets (or the risk of assets) off the balance sheet of the originator via an outright sale to an SPV or the originator's purchasing credit default protection from an SPV.

The annual gross issuance volume of CDOs worldwide grew more than tenfold from USD 48.1 billion in 1997 to a historic record of USD 520.6 billion by the end of 2006 (before collapsing to USD 61.9 and USD 4.3 billion in 2007 and 2008 as investors abandoned the market and primary issuance came to a halt, see Figure 1). Given its rapid growth before the credit crisis, market data on securitisation activity in both the United States and Europe suggest that CDOs contributed to almost 50 percent of global issuance of securitized debt during the years 2006 and 2007. Synthetic transactions also became the predominant type of CDOs over the years. During the heyday of the CDO market, two-thirds of new issues deals were synthetic: USD 340.4 billion cash flow CDOs vs. USD 92.8 billion funded synthetic CDOs (with the rest accounted for by market value transactions). This compares with one out of twenty in 1997: USD 45.5 billion cash in CDOs vs. USD 2.7 billion funded synthetic CDOs. Currently, CDO issuance stands at USD 6.4 billion, of which almost all transactions are cash flow-based.

Despite their popularity in mature markets (and the recent fall from grace during the US sub-prime crisis), CDOs have not been applied widely in emerging markets. Whenever emerging market obligations are included in CDOs, they are usually sovereign or quasi-sovereign bonds, given (i) the limited number of issuers in the emerging market universe, (ii) the high proportions of debt accounted for by sovereign borrowers, and (iii) the paucity of CDS contracts on emerging market corporates. Nonetheless, several key CDOs on emerging market sovereigns and corporates should be mentioned by name. One was Citigroup's Global EM CDO hard-currency emerging market sovereign debt in October 2006. This was followed soon by the Evolution EM CDO,[5] which was the first of its kind to provide investors with full capital structure exposure to a diverse global pool of local currency-denominated debt of emerging market sovereign obligors. Another was the Sphaera EM CDO in December 2005,[6] which was designed as a balance sheet exercise to transfer some of the credit risk associated with Citigroup's own emerging market loan portfolio. CDO technology has been applied to other asset classes in emerging markets, such as microfinance loans, only shortly before the credit crisis. After having stalled for more than two years, the market for microfinance CDOs is now starting a modest comeback.

The first microfinance CDO was issued in 2004 (and repeated in 2005) by the Geneva-based microfinance investment consultancy BlueOrchard Finance S.A. in cooperation with the U.S. investment advisory group Developing World Markets.[7] In April 2006, BlueOrchard Finance S.A. together with Morgan Stanley went on to launch the first public microloan CDO (BlueOrchard Loans for Development 2006-1 or BOLD 2006-1). This vehicle provided a fixed-rate, five-year notional funding of USD 99.1 million to a diversified group of 21 MFIs in 13 developing countries: Albania, Azerbaijan, Bolivia, Bosnia and Herzegovina, Cambodia, Colombia, Ecuador, Georgia, Mexico, Mongolia, Nicaragua, Peru, and Russia.

5 Subsequent to the initial EM CDO transaction, in April 2007 Citigroup issued another three-year synthetic EM CDO on a portfolio of USD 450 million worth of local currency sovereign debt in Emerald Capital Series 2007-1.

6 Deutsche Bank Global Markets emulated Citigroup's foray into structuring exposures to corporate emerging market obligors in June 2006 when it completed the closure of a USD 500 million emerging markets collateralised loan obligation (CLO) (CRAFT EM CLO 2006-1). A CLO is a CDO with loans as underlying reference assets.

7 Following this transaction, the consultancy company Symbiotics and the European Investment Fund (EIF) structured a CLO referencing a MFI network in 2005.

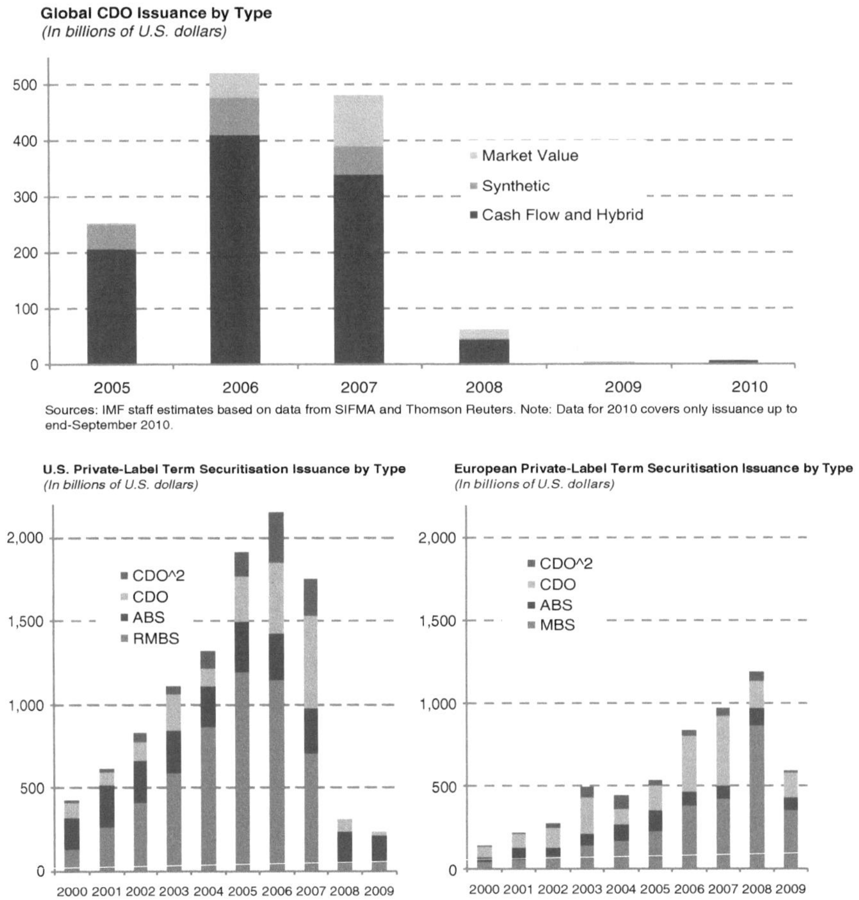

Sources: IMF staff estimates based on data from SIFMA and Thomson Reuters. Note: Data for 2010 covers only issuance up to end-September 2010.

Sources: IMF staff estimates based on data from JPMorgan Chase & Co., Board of Governors of the Federal Reserve Systems, Inside Mortgage Finance, Merrill Lynch, the Association for Financial Markets in Europe (AFME), the European Covered Bond Council (ECBC), and Fitch ratings.
Note: ABS = asset-backed security; CDO = collateralised debt obligation; CDO^2 = collateralised debt obligation-squared and CDOs backed by ABS and MBS; MBS = mortgage-backed security; RMBS = residential MBS.

Fig. 1. Global private label securitisation issuance

At the time, BOLD 2006-1 was the single largest commercial investment in the history of microfinance. Since 20 percent of the loan portfolio's asset notional value was denominated in local currencies (other than U.S. Dollars and Euros), five-year foreign exchange rate swaps were used to hedge currency movements on the subordination of the transaction until the maturity date. The entire subordinated note class was underwritten by FMO, the Dutch Development Finance Company, whose willingness to accept the equity or "first loss" position of the transaction attracted interest from private investors.

In 2006, Symbiotics and Global Partnerships designed the first rated microfinance CDO before Morgan Stanley issued another series of synthetic CLO notes (BOLD 2007-1). The CDO had a three-tier structure made up of micro-loans to raise USD 108 million for MFIs that lend to more than 70,000 borrowers.[8] The average interest rate was 8.5 percent. Unlike the previous issue, this transaction was partially rated[9] which widened the number of investors that could assume exposure to small loans in emerging market countries.

Further building on growing investor confidence in structured microfinance credit, Deutsche Bank's Microfinance-Invest Nr. 1 CDO in September 2007, with KfW as lead investor, was the first global microfinance transaction where private, commercial investors invested in unrated first loss (100 percent) and mezzanine tranches (65 percent).[10] This transaction helped annual gross issuance exceed the USD 4 billion mark in 2007, which remains the high watermark of the microfinance CDO market to date (and barely below the USD 4.3 billion total global issuance of the CDO market after the credit crisis in 2009). As of this writing, a USD 21.2 million transaction sponsored by Finca International, a U.S.-based microfinance institution, in collaboration with Deutsche Bank, represents one of the most recent efforts to rehabilitate the CDO market for structured microfinance.[11]

Considerations for Innovation

The following section examines important constraints on financial innovation and highlights opportunities for widening the scope of structured finance in emerging market and developing countries as lenders search for new ways to access capital. Areas of interest include technical improvement, asset diversity, and market access. This section also shows how structured finance can support local capital market development, diversify investment in largely unexplored areas of economic activity, and expand the spectrum of financing options for development purposes.

---

8 The BOLD programme provided funding to participating MFIs in Azerbaijan, Bosnia and Herzegovina, Cambodia, Colombia, Georgia, Ghana, Kenya, Mongolia, Montenegro, Nicaragua, Peru, Russia, and Serbia.

9 The senior and mezzanine tranches with notional amounts of USD 48 million and USD 12 million were rated "AA" and "BBB" by Standard and Poor's respectively, while USD 50 million remained unrated.

10 The issue was backed by subordinated, medium-term loans to 21 MFIs in 15 countries on four continents.

11 Interestingly, with most CDO issuance having been shelved in light of inexpensive central bank funding since the height of the credit crisis, these modest signs of recovery in the microfinance CDO segment have become more significant economically. In 2009, this transaction represented 0.5 percent of global CDO issuance.

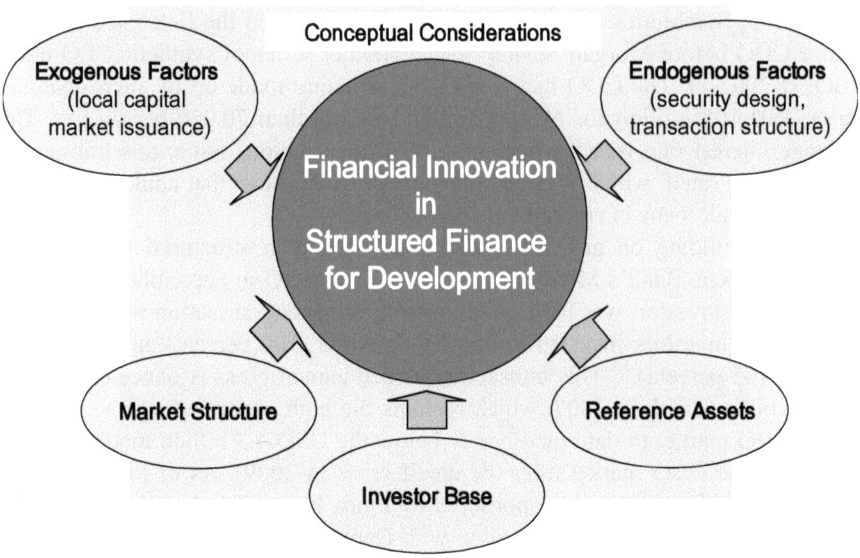

Fig. 2. Conceptual framework for financial innovation in structured finance for development.

Conceptual Considerations

Structured finance offers issuers considerable flexibility to create securities with distinct risk-return profiles in maturity structure, security design, and asset type. Structured finance instruments facilitate the unbundling, transformation and diversification of financial risks. These risks can be customised to the preferences and tolerances of agents, improving the capacity of the financial system to bear risk and intermediate capital. Such risk diversification should, in principle, improve the pricing and managing of risk and enhance the allocation of capital within the financial system. Any new applications of structured finance are driven by the prospect of obtaining additional rents from offering superior risk-return propositions that suit individual investors' appetites while establishing benchmark transactions that build investor maturity. Depending on the degree of replicability, such innovation paves the way for the more efficient execution of future transactions with similar characteristics.

However, financial innovations might escape regulatory oversight and increase financial sector vulnerabilities. Potential adverse consequences may be severe in many developing economies with small local capital markets. The increasing complexity of the structured finance market, together with its ever growing range of products, creates challenges for governance and information dissemination. With the increasing sophistication of financial products amid a greater diversity of financial institutions and the growing interdependence of financial markets, vulnerabilities are likely to be found where market forces and participants are left to their own devices. In some instances, structured finance creates incentive structures, such as leveraged security designs and tranche subordination,[12] which could encourage greater risk-taking in a benign economic environment with adverse economic consequences when stress occurs. Greater moral hazard and the danger that risks can become concentrated in a few large financial institutions complicate crisis resolution and intensify potential systemic vulnerabilities that extend across institutions and national boundaries.

Against this background, infrastructural characteristics that ensure market integrity and collective interest during times of stress are critical. This is especially important when self-governing crisis resolution seems to be no more than a faintly compelling proposition to limit the adverse externalities of market failure. Despite greater macroeconomic stability and financial liberalisation, many countries lack the regulatory framework, disclosure standards, and centralised burden sharing – through capital rules and other statutory and prudential provisions – to manage these contingencies in a pro-active manner.

The troubled evolution of structured finance testifies to the inherent risks of financial innovation, which have to be acknowledged with the same alacrity as its economic benefits. The market turbulence in the wake of the U.S. subprime market meltdown underscores the importance of reliable valuation of structured finance products. They also highlight the possible spread effects of the structured finance market on other investment classes as asset shocks move across capital market segments.

As concerns about subprime mortgages increased with mounting defaults during the first half of 2007, doubts surfaced about the quality and pricing of CDOs and other high-yield structured finance instruments that were used to refinance the origination of these mortgages. It became clear that the market prices of these credit-sensitive assets were inflated by excessive sourcing of subprime mortgages and related claims that were included in these structured finance instruments. As the credit cycle began to turn, deteriorating asset quality and dwindling investor demand led to a general repricing of risk. In addition, funding structures with maturity mismatches (i.e., short-term ABCP issuance for long-term mortgage loans) proved to be fragile and amplified declining investor confidence.

A comprehensive and reliable framework for the risk assessment of structured products hinges on efficient price formation in transparent markets with standard market practices, prudential regulation, and enhanced disclosure at both the product and issuer level. The rating process has to account for mismatches (in currency

[12] However, the subordination structure of many securitisation transactions concentrates expected losses in a small first-loss position, shifting most unexpected risk to more senior tranches (Jobst, 2005). The ratio of unexpected to expected losses of each tranche increases with seniority. This subordinated security design – with risk concentration in junior investments and leveraged exposure to marginal changes in unexpected loss for senior investors – complicates valuation of contingent claims in times of stress when asset volatility increases.

and maturity), extreme asset price dynamics and joint movements of distinct sources of market risk, credit risk, and liquidity risk. Off-balance sheet constructions and risk-and-reward transfers make it important to revisit how prudential reporting can be improved so that the potential risk is better captured. Regulators must be satisfied regarding the adequacy of prudential capital requirements and the adequacy of liquidity arrangements under "worst case" scenarios. Consequently, if a market is expected to function without stresses from price corrections and sudden shifts in investor sentiment, much greater disclosure is required regarding the risks contained within complex products.[13]

Exogenous Factors: Market Impediments to Direct Securitisation in Local Capital Markets

Structured finance is a promising channel for producing local fixed-income securities in ways that overcome local capital market constraints by turning investments with high credit risks into relatively high-grade securities. In this regard, securitisation may play a role in the cost-efficient and expedient funding of ambitious infrastructure projects, retail mortgage lending, and long-term productive investment by small- and medium-size enterprises (SMEs).

Asset securitisation has evolved into a widely-used capital market-based structured funding mechanism in many developed countries to mitigate market imperfections and financing constraints. However, access to structured finance in emerging markets remains limited. Local securitised issuance is sponsored mainly by the most creditworthy private originators and public sector agencies and the potential of development finance to sustain profitable structured finance often goes unnoticed. In the case of "indirect" microfinance securitisation, foreign sourcing of emerging market assets via synthetic CDO structures does little to promote local market development in ways that create a more efficient financial system.

Several impediments block more extensive use of local asset securitisation. Inconsistent market practices, deficient supervisory standards, and insufficient market transparency due to weak rating agencies are at fault. They have encumbered the emergence of a mature investor base, a sound credit culture, and collateral enforcement for investor protection within a tried and tested regulatory framework. Difficulties associated with the sourcing and structuring of eligible asset classes with a sufficient degree of diversification and the paucity of historical information

[13] As financial intermediation in emerging markets becomes more balanced and competitive as a result of greater capital market sophistication, the macro-financial linkages are also likely to change, often with major implications for policy makers. The influence of monetary policy on interest rates and the real economy depends critically on the structure of the financial system. Different forms of financial innovation, such as asset securitisation, have the potential to permanently alter the transmission mechanism of monetary policy and, through consumption and investment decisions, their influence on the real economy.

about default and recovery rates complicate the assessment of counterparty and credit risk in emerging markets and have resulted in diverse origination standards.

Securitised debt in emerging markets is supplied through a mix of private placements and public issues due to regulatory constraints. The combination of pent-up local demand and diverse origination standards has also dampened higher growth and created few incentives for secondary market trading. Finally, there are still considerable constraints on foreign investor participation and more diversified demand from local investors. Advancement has been retarded by inadequate reforms of unfunded pension systems and the restrictive statutory investment requirements of banks, insurance companies, and mutual funds.

Box 3. Essential Requirements for Securitisation in Local Capital Markets

The efficient execution of structured finance depends on an adequate and bankable regulatory framework. Such a framework includes legal provisions for bankruptcy, tax, and corporate governance issues related to the contractual obligations of agents, especially as regards reliable dispute resolution mechanisms. The prudent execution of authorisation and disclosure requirements are also required, as well as transparent transaction structures that ensure demonstrable and unimpeded control over collateral, subject to persistent monitoring of asset performance by rating agencies, trustees, and guarantors.

The feasibility of creating a sustainable securitisation market requires the presence of additional economic and infrastructural conditions along with sound market practices. These include (i) a good credit culture, (ii) information transparency through standardised reporting, (iii) diverse asset supply and relative asset price competitiveness against other sources of external finance, (iv) sufficient domestic savings and sophisticated institutional investors to manage these savings professionally, (v) an infrastructure of arrangers, clearing agents, exchanges, market makers, as well as (vi) professional credit rating agencies that establish consistent standards for risk measurement and valuation across a wide range of transaction features and security designs.

Some of these teething issues are likely to be resolved in a sequenced transition towards more information transparency, asset-class diversity, and greater capital market sophistication. This has to accompany regulatory reforms, financial liberalisation, and a mature local investor base. Infrastructural and legal shortcomings are the biggest test for emerging market securitisation. Legal frameworks for securitisation are still at an early stage of development across emerging markets. In some instances, the absence of securitisation laws has allowed issuers to adopt less stringent regulations on conventional debt securities without regulatory incentives guiding good governance, and risk management without collective provisions that minimise potential threats to financial stability.

Endogenous Factors: Security Design and Risk Management – Evidence from Structured Finance in Emerging Markets

Besides economic, infrastructural and legal challenges, considerations of security design and risk management play a crucial role when structured finance is applied to illiquid and non-standardised asset classes without secondary market prices. Although many aspects in the following section are based on recent evidence from structured microfinance, they offer general lessons for structured finance in emerging markets and its potential to facilitate development finance.

Management of Market Imperfections

Investor subordination serves as an essential mechanism to prevent or mitigate agency costs from adverse selection and market segmentation/incompleteness due to imperfect capital markets. In an emerging market context, high execution costs, structural complexity, as well as heightened administration, collection, and fraud risks warrant careful consideration. These can amplify the potential for problems where, originators hold an information advantage over the typical investor regarding the credit quality of the securitised portfolio. This "lemons phenomena" à la Akerlof (1970) is likely to be particularly relevant when the information advantage associated with opaque asset classes is considerable, such as for microloans or infrastructure projects.

A subordinated security design solves this problem by supplying less informed investors with safe tranches with low default probabilities, while the originators or more sophisticated investors retain the riskier, more junior tranches. Moreover, tranching has value if markets are incomplete or segmented. These features are due either to investment restrictions dictated by investor traditions or mandates and government regulations that render certain assets unattainable, or by the limited supply of certain categories of debt instruments that have risk-return profiles that could be replicated or enhanced by securitisation.[14]

Equity Ownership and Integrated Risk Mitigants

Selling equity tranches has become less prevalent as the structured finance market matures. However, to signal credit quality it is still not uncommon for the issuer to retain the residual claim in a new asset class or securitisation structure as a low-cost risk sharing and support mechanism. An equity claim absorbs a credit loss before any principal of investor-held tranches is written down. The absence of long default histories in emerging market countries, uncertain recovery rate estimates due to untested collateral enforcement procedures, and relatively high sys-

[14] Tranching can also generate arbitrage profits. This is achieved by creating a subordinated capital structure that pools assets having individual rating-based prices that may deviate from the fair market valuation.

temic risk in loan portfolios (such as in microfinance),[15] requires an originator bank to retain a relatively high "first loss" or "equity" tranche. The level would typically range from 15 to 30 percent versus the two to five percent typical in mature markets, and/or higher levels of subordination.

Development institutions such as IFC and FMO have taken equity stakes in such transactions to attract participation by global investment banks as arrangers administering the underwriting process. Equity is usually supplemented by the over-collateralisation of receivables, permanent debt service reserve accounts, and cash flows from excess spread which are blocked to ensure the originator's compliance with contractual obligations to repay investors.[16] Moreover, recourse agreements with originators establish legal grounds for firm asset control on securitised receivables in case a third-party guarantee is called.[17] In addition, project grading in concessional development finance can help improve overall credit quality.

Default Risk and Recovery Rates

The scrutiny of securitised assets is generally less accurate in emerging markets compared to developed countries. This is due to the comparative paucity of historical data on defaults, which hinders reliable estimates for recovery rates used in pricing and rating tranched products. In particular, relatively inexperienced analysts at rating agencies and underwriters might escalate the risks posed by spotty data on underlying assets to the structural integrity of certain securitisation trans-

[15] Since structured microfinance obligations are typically collateralised by assets from multiple lenders, they largely eliminate idiosyncratic risk by spreading it over different countries or markets. Moreover, they fund very small enterprises, whose economic activity satisfies the inelastic, basic demand of consumers. However, pooled MFI portfolios might be increasingly susceptible to marginal changes in the correlation of non-diversifiable structural factors, such as adverse movements in exchange rates, economic growth, or inflation expectations across different countries, which impact the valuation portfolio assets. Diversification gains might also be offset by the increasing risk that MFIs may abandon their traditional lending strategy in the search for greater profitability in urban areas or different client groups. An improvement of risk diversification could be achieved in mixed portfolios consisting of SME and microloans.

[16] As a mechanism of protecting note holders, excess spread in Citigroup's 2006 Evolution EM CDO realises reverse subordination of issued notes. If the aggregate U.S. dollar par value drops below the initial notional amount, subordination is eroded. The constituent notes are written down in reverse order for the purpose of calculating principal outstanding and the payment of interest and principal over time and at maturity. Interest is trapped inside the structure to re-build par. In contrast to conventional transactions, any foreign currency appreciation during the maturity term results in a "re-filling" of the subordination structure.

[17] In the BRAC structured microfinance transaction, the issuer also committed itself to replace all non-performing loans underlying the trust structure.

actions. Moreover, the "cloud of country risk uncertainty" overshadows the analysis of specific credit risks.

Rating agencies use very conservative assumptions for recovery rates of securitised emerging market assets, which explain the low volume of these deal types due to additional capital cost (Chavee et al., 2007, Fox et al., 2007). Contemporary transaction structures provide recovery insurance to make the capital structure more efficient and achieve high ratings on the most senior tranches of the transaction. For instance, Citigroup's Sphaera EM CDO fixed the recovery rate of exposures at 40 percent, which eliminated uncertainty about adequate recovery rates in the pricing process and simplified the overall analysis.

Rating and Investor Base

Repackaging and slicing the proceeds from the securitised assets into a security design of subordinated tranches with varying levels of risk can raise the credit quality high enough to make senior notes viable for mainstream institutional investors even if the transaction remains unrated. Nevertheless, the absence of ratings frequently restricts institutional investment subject to statutory requirements. Large and unrated parts of securitised portfolios are likely to be retained by the issuer. This is unlike other emerging market collateral, such as corporate loans and sovereign debt, for which risk assessment methodologies based on existing historical information are more advanced. And most highly, investment grade rated tranches are publicly placed.

The traditional investor base of individuals and foundations is broadening slowly as performance data on emerging market assets gradually accumulates. Deal monitoring is at an early stage of market development. Ratings are an important step in broadening investor participation and in substantiating assumptions about default risk and asset correlation. Transactions involving emerging market exposures are usually benchmarked against a financial model. Whenever trades are proposed, the manager will benchmark the proposed transaction against the model to determine whether the investment is sensible and within the contractual limits of the management agreement. Structured finance ratings of these models should be based on:

- an assessment of the eligibility criteria applicable to the selected exposures to control credit and foreign exchange risk;
- the credit quality of the counterparty, if applicable;
- protection against losses on principal and interest payments;
- the quality of portfolio management; and
- the legal and structural integrity of the issuance.

Legal Certainty and Structural Flexibility from Synthetic Structures

The synthetic transfer of credit risk can overcome several key obstacles to the securitisation of emerging market assets. Synthetic transactions customise capital structure exposure, which increases the efficiency of transaction and rating status. They also offer issuers the flexibility to seek credit protection from two different modes of investor participation – through either "funded" Collateralised Loan Notes (CLNs) or "unfunded" Credit Default Swaps (CDSs) – with little or no up-front payment.

In this way, issuers sidestep regulatory uncertainties in emerging markets and the legal complexities of dealing with multi-jurisdictional portfolios and their problems. CLNs and CDSs can be issued within a well-established framework using standard market practices for greater clarity and risk assessment, especially regarding the definition of "credit events"[18] which determine CDO cash flows. Defaulted emerging market credits tend to be held for longer periods than similar exposures in mature market countries. This reflects the illiquidity and the difficulty of bankruptcy workouts, which might still place the subjective "materiality" requirement over the theoretically more objective criteria based on reference entity creditworthiness.

Synthetic securitisation is also beneficial in many civil law countries where the transfer is legal title is complicated by more stringent property laws. Within these jurisdictions the cumbersome and lengthy processes of debtor notification creates significant obstacles to the perfection of security interest in bankruptcy remote structures.[19] While synthetic transactions help overcome this constraint, they generally require credit ratings of the underlying obligations and credit loss histories so that default risk can be verified for the design of investment mandates and hedging strategies. Both are difficult in the emerging market context as noted above, given the informational difficulties that arise in trying to structure credit derivatives covering "multiple-name" emerging market credits.

Foreign Exchange Risk

Local currency exposure tends to inhibit securitisation activity, mainly because foreign exchange risk has the potential to dilute the effect of credit enhancement through subordination, i.e., protection against losses through the sequential nature

---

[18] The standard "credit events" that trigger payment under emerging market credit derivative contracts are (i) failure to pay, (ii) repudiation/moratorium, (iii) obligation, (iv) acceleration, and (v) restructuring.

[19] The robustness of the transaction to bankruptcy proceedings requires that (i) securitised assets have been absolutely transferred from the originator to the SPV, so that they are detached from the bankruptcy estate (usually referred to as true sale), and (ii) originator and SPV are separate entities so that the assets and liabilities of the latter would not be substantively consolidated with the originator in the event of insolvency proceedings (commonly referred to as substantive non-consolidation).

of principal payments.[20] As an alternative to standard hedging via foreign exchange swaps over a fixed maturity term, some issuers provide additional protection through the diversion of interest due on subordinated notes (i.e., excess spread). This device traps interest payments inside the transaction structure whenever the reference portfolio's notional hard currency value declines in response to local currency depreciation. Furthermore, the rollover and amortising character of a transaction allows guarantors to mitigate their currency risk if a transaction can be periodically renewed and if all parties so desire. In the case of the BRAC transaction, FMO and KfW acted as guarantors and structuring investors. They circumvented high country risk by using local currency only instead of denominating the securitised debt in foreign currency.

Commercial Viability

Structured microfinance has a distinct profit proposition. It relies on arbitrage gains from a cost of carry below the returns from funding MFI lending. As the microfinance industry matures, competition among MFIs and infrastructural improvements such as "branchless banking" are expected to reduce interest rates. But there remains the question whether microfinance lending beyond a concentrated, urban clientele is feasible without subsidies that offset the high risks and administrative costs.

Other Structural Improvements

The rising popularity of structured microfinance also highlights areas where existing formats and security designs can be optimised, supplemented with additional features, or replaced with alternative transaction or payment structures. These include:

- different forms of funding and collateralisation, through donors or compulsory deposits to ensure repayment;
- variation of loss and recovery projections based on different incentive schemes underlying the microloan origination process (group lending or individual lending) using progressive disbursement;
- using the super-senior tranche concept of KfW synthetic securitisation platform; and
- alternative funding through asset-backed commercial paper (ABCP).[21]

---

[20] If there are any ex ante interest rate or currency mismatches between the securitised underlying risks and liabilities, the issuer is usually required to enter into interest rate or foreign exchange swaps to hedge those risks.

[21] An ABCP conduit is a special purpose entity (SPE) that issues commercial paper and uses the proceeds to purchase short-term assets (e.g., trade receivables, credit card receivables, auto and equipment leases) and long-term assets (e.g., mortgage-backed securities, commercial loans, collateralised bond obligations, and collateralised loan obligations).

The latter is a useful tool to help issuers improve the balance sheet and capital management, and which is a means of diversifying funding sources by attracting a new investor base.

Innovations for New Markets and Investors

Financial innovation should also create a balanced and diverse supply and demand. To date, most structured finance for development is limited to a small set of eligible asset classes which are arranged, managed and issued by a few, well-known entities. However, diversified supply is critical in creating asset price competition in a wide and liquid structured finance market. A small number of repeat issuers create originator concentration risk and stymies asset price competition. While the backing by a handful of large, well-known issuers might provide investor comfort, the diversification of asset classes across a wider range of deal types is highly desirable. In some instances, transaction structures have been slightly modified to suit the legal, regulatory and infrastructural requirements of other jurisdictions, such as the creation of a secondary mortgage market in Russia.

Moreover, a concentrated investor base and deficient local capital market development limits funding possibilities, especially if investment from foreign (institutional) investors in these markets is subject to capital account restrictions.

Given the dominance of banks and other large institutional investors, more balanced demand would require the development of structures and mechanisms that encourage greater retail participation. Deutsche Bank's recent db Microfinance Invest Nr. 1 CDO demonstrated that the "democratisation of microfinance" is possible, opening investment opportunities for private individuals for the first time in structured microfinance. In emerging market countries, Korea's experience in creating what has become the world's largest equity derivatives exchange might also be instructive. KOFEX, the national derivative exchange, has been very successful in attracting retail investors with the help of internet-based trading. It offers relatively simple derivative products to retail investors at low transaction costs and small margin requirements amid a favourable legal and regulatory framework.

The payments that are collected from the purchased assets are used to redeem the commercial paper at maturity. There are two types of ABCP conduits: single-seller and multi-seller. In a single-seller conduit, all of the assets originate from a single company, and generally all of the assets will be of the same type. In a multi-seller conduit, any number of companies may be originating and selling assets to the conduit, and the variety of assets within the conduit's portfolio can vary widely. Multi-seller conduits are generally sponsored by large commercial banks.

Innovations for New Reference Asset Classes: Islamic Microfinance Securitisation

The need for infrastructure investment and local capital market development is most acute in those countries where financial transactions are subject to *shari'ah* law, which requires asset transfer and risk sharing that implies automatic collateralisation. Given established microfinance securitisation methodologies, structured finance for development purposes could be readily applied to shari'ah-compliant transaction structures either on the back of existing Islamic microfinance programs, or by Islamic securitisation in the form of shari'ah-compliant investment certificates, or *Sukuk*.

The most popular form of securitised credit in Islamic finance is commonly referred to as Sukuk, which is structured in a way that is similar to conventional asset-backed securities (ABS). Sukuk are asset-backed wholesale instruments that are structured to comply with shari'ah, which, among other provisions, prohibits the receipt and payment of interest. Islamic law stipulates that income must be derived from an underlying real business risk rather than as a guaranteed return from a loan. As such, Sukuk investors own the underlying asset(s) via a special purpose vehicle (SPV), which funds unsecured payments to investors from direct investment in real, religiously-sanctioned economic activity (Wilson, 2005). Sukuk commoditise the proceeds from profitable asset transfers between capital providers and users in different Islamic finance contracts. Sukuk transform capital gains into marketable securities. The capital gains are created by bilateral risk sharing between borrowers and lenders in shari'ah-compliant lending transactions in the form of an instalment sale, or trust-based investments in existing or future assets. Sukuk usually refinance the assets of one or a combination of three basic forms of Islamic finance – synthetic loans (*murabahah*), sale-leasebacks (*ijara*), or profit-sharing arrangements (*musharakah* or *mudharabah*).[22]

In recent years there has been a surge in the issuance of Islamic securities by corporates and public sector entities amid strong demand for alternative investments. Gross issuance quadrupled from USD 7.2 billion in 2004 to close to USD 39 billion by the end of 2007, owing in large part to enabling capital market regulations, a favourable macroeconomic environment, large infrastructure development plans in some Middle Eastern economies (IOSCO, 2008). However, Sukuk have not escaped unscathed from the credit crisis. By 2008, Sukuk volumes contracted sharply as a result of challenging market conditions, liquidity constraints, and the presentation of new rules on the shari'ah compliance of Sukuk (Jobst et al., 2008). In particular, the less supportive economic environment in the Gulf Corporation Council (GCC) countries and the regional real estate sector troubled by the slowdown of global trade and foreign direct investment have contributed to this development. Amid a gradual normalization of credit conditions in early

[22] The Accounting and Auditing Organization of Islamic Finance Institutions (AAOIF) recognises 14 types of sukuk.

2009, incipient demand in tandem with a greater sovereign issuance helped stabilize the primary market for Sukuk. In 2009, global Sukuk sales exceeded USD 25 billion, up from USD 17.2 billion in 2008. On the assumption of a stable rate of growth, the volume of Sukuk issued by governments and corporates is expected to regain traction over the medium term, spurred by demand especially from banks, insurance companies and pension funds in countries where Sukuk are emerging as an attractive diversification tool to the equity and real estate markets.

Sukuk issuance can offer a straightforward capital cost advantage due to a potentially broader investor base and its asset-backed structure. Sukuk tend to be bought at a premium over conventional bonds of similar maturity. This can be the result of specific investment interests, such as shari'ah compliance of the transaction

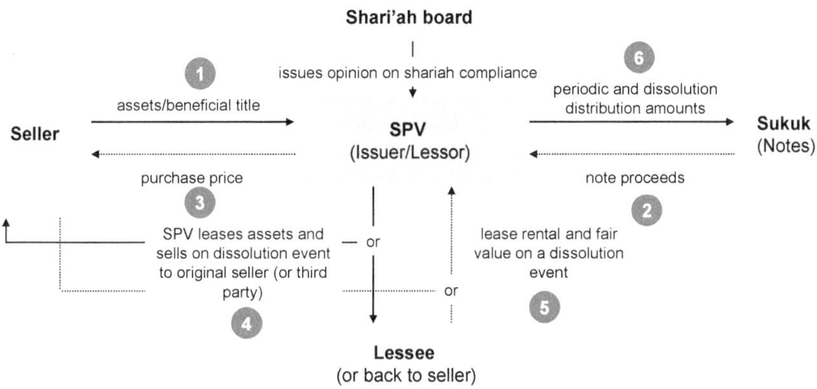

Fig. 3. A simple *Al-ijara (thumma al-bay) Sukuk* structure at work.[23]

or hedge funds seeking asset returns uncorrelated to conventional fixed income assets. In addition, the asset-backed nature of Sukuk implies that a higher credit rating can be achieved for a Sukuk structure than from standard bond finance, potentially lowering the cost of capital.

However, administrative and legal considerations can lead to additional costs. The initial structuring and issuance costs of Sukuk are likely to be higher than those of a standard security. Since Islamic principles require direct asset ownership by creditors, specific cash flows from real assets have to be identified to support the structure. Such deals are more likely to be related to particular projects and programmes, thereby increasing the lead time to prepare an issue. Also the question surrounding the enforceability of investor interest under Islamic jurisprudence still contains considerable legal uncertainty, given the potential of Islamic

[23] Under this arrangement the underlying assets are sold by the issuer to a SPV and leased back for the duration of the project (Jobst et al., 2007).

jurisprudence to invalidate perfected security interests (under commercial law) on the grounds of full recourse to the originator.

Carbon Securitisation

In light of the rapid growth in trading volumes of carbon emission rights worldwide, carbon instruments could generate considerable interest in emerging market countries as a potential asset class for development-enhancing securitisation (Ali, 2007; Borod and Tan, 2006).[24] Demand for carbon emission rights has been driven by the companies that need to offset against actual carbon emissions, such as carbon dioxide and other greenhouse gases, in order to meet regulatory limits.[25] This growing demand – whether for compliance or investment purposes – would allow many emerging market countries to embrace securitisation in order to raise funds based on their inventories of carbon instruments.

Carbon instruments are fundamentally different from the vast majority of assets that have been securitised so far. As a non-financial asset, emission rights do not amortise in the manner of trade receivables, mortgage loans or credit card balances. Similar to inventory securitisation, any cash flows that are necessary to service securities are generated from resale of a portfolio of underlying assets, which is drawn down over the life of the transaction.[26] Since inventory securitisation is subject to pricing risks, eligible types of collateral must satisfy the following criteria:

- the market for the investor is regulated (with high entry barriers, so supply is scarce);
- there is an organised secondary market; and
- inventory is freely available, liquid and durable.

---

[24] The launch of the European Climate Change Programme (EECCP) in 2000 has led to the adoption of the Emissions Trading System (ETS), the European Union's key tool for reducing greenhouse gas emissions and the world's first carbon dioxide trading scheme. In 2009, EUR 89 billion worth of allowances were traded in the EU ETS, more than ten times of its first year trading 2005 of EUR 9.4 billion.

[25] The main types of carbon instruments are EU Emissions Allowance Units (EAUs) under the EU ETS and the Certified Emission Reductions (CERs) produced under the Kyoto Protocol's Clean Development Mechanism.

[26] Inventory securitisation structures can be adapted to carbon instruments via true sale or whole business structures. In the case of true sale securitisation, the originator sells assets to the SPV, which refinances the purchase by issuing securities to investors without recourse to the originator or exposure to the credit risk of the originator. In whole business structures, the SPV uses the proceeds from issuing securities to issue a collateralised loan secured by the underlying inventory. Investors remain exposed to credit risk and also have the benefit of recourse against the originator.

Carbon instruments generally meet these conditions. However, some uncertainty surrounding the legal nature of carbon instruments (personal rights vs. property rights) has limited the transferability and convertibility of such instruments into perfected security interests.

The commercialisation of carbon instruments via securitisation would facilitate sustainable industrial production, especially in developing countries where proceeds from forward sale of emission rights reduce funding constraints. Moreover, the potential of foreign investment to generate valuable assets in the form of project-specific Emission Reduction Units (ERU) can facilitate profitable infrastructure investment in emerging market and developing countries alike. In addition, project receivables can be monetised through securitisation.

Renewable Energy and Energy Efficiency Securitisation

Renewable energy certificates (RECs) could also be used as collateral to structured finance. A REC represents the value of attributes of electricity generated from renewable energy sources, which are unbundled from the value of commodity electricity. RECs are sold or traded separately in response to the challenge of verifying the fuel mix and emissions data claimed by electric service providers. They also facilitate transactions across regional boundaries and reduce transmission costs because they are not subject to the geographic constraints of the commodity electricity. Instead, purchasers can acquire rights to lowest-cost renewable energy attributes regardless of where the RECs are generated. Since RECs rely on market forces to distribute benefits to those who value them most, the market for RECs offers a pricing mechanism for the efficient production and consumption of electricity.

Some renewable energy developers in the United States have begun to sell forward the future value of RECs generated from new or planned renewable energy projects to retail customers. This enables developers to front-load expected project revenues and enhances their ability to fund and complete new projects within a shorter time period. If used in structured finance, energy producers would monetise expected proceeds from selling either the bundled energy and RECs or RECs alone to a refinancing conduit. Securitisation of RECs facilitates the unbundling, transformation and diversification of price risk associated with renewable energy generation.

RECs have quickly become the currency of renewable energy markets in mature economies because of their flexibility and the absence of geographic or physical limitations of commodity electricity. There are two distinct markets for RECs: (i) the compliance market, mandated by state-level Renewable Portfolio Standards (RPS), and the voluntary market, in which companies and institutions purchase certificates. In the United States, utilities and marketers use RECs, bundled with electricity in retail products, to supply renewable energy products to end-use consumers in the "voluntary market." They also comply with renewable portfolio standards (RPS) and other regulatory requirements and government mandates in the "compliance market."

Compliance markets have the largest potential to support structured finance products aimed at funding the development of new renewable energy resources. In countries where authorities have adopted provisions to ensure that the development of new renewable sources of energy is guided by RPS policies, the commercialisation of RECs promises to have the greatest impact,[27] with REC being commonly purchased wholesale within bundled renewable energy products. However, voluntary markets provide insufficient security for project finance. The short-term nature of most voluntary purchases makes it exceedingly difficult for developers to finance new renewable energy projects to increase supply. This reflects the uncertainty of future demand and the possible unwillingness of lenders or investors to rely on voluntary demand as security for financing. Sourcing RECs into structured products might also help originators overcome difficulties in selling unbundled RECs to residential consumers in voluntary markets due to the intricate and intangible characteristics of RECs.

Participation in carbon emission markets could expand the scope of funding renewable energy. Although RECs are not eligible to participate in many cases, greater recognition of the emission-reduction benefits of renewable energy and their inclusion in government sanctioned allowance allocations are imminent. Nonetheless, it remains questionable whether the carbon market – at the current stage of development – provides a sufficient guarantee of future revenues to satisfy the funding needs of project developers and the collateral requirements of structured finance transactions.

Nonetheless, the lack of exchanges, forward markets, and price indices challenges the sustainability of RECs and their application in structured finance due to market risk. Even advanced compliance markets in the United States (Aulisi and Hanson, 2004) and Europe (EU Directive, 2001) are still very illiquid and deficient in market infrastructure to track and verify REC transactions. They are also mired in legal uncertainty on the part of lenders or equity investors unless REC ownership is specified in contracts between qualifying facilities and utilities. Furthermore, difficulties in communicating the concept of an REC to industry participants, including generators, electricity providers, regulators, and consumers may limit the effectiveness of efforts to market claims supporting the environmental benefits of stand-alone RECs and to residential consumers.

Measures to ameliorate these concerns about RECs as collateral for structured finance are predicated on the creation of stable demand. For REC trading to reach a critical mass and produce sufficient revenue streams if sold forward, large insti-

[27] In the United States, the compliance market is currently about four times the size of the voluntary market and is projected to grow by more than 50 percent by 2015, with REC sales reaching an estimated 179 million MWh. In a forecast scenario that includes passage of a Renewable Portfolio Standard at the U.S. federal level, the REC market could overall grow nearly triple in size to 329 million MWh by 2015. Market prices differ between voluntary and compliance markets, as well as by region, resource type, vintage, and volume. In general, REC prices tend to be higher in the latter market, especially in supply-constrained regions.

tutions and corporate buyers would have to be willing to hold long positions to hedge against the price risk of renewable energy. Aside from renewable energy funds offering price floors as insurance against uncertain future markets, national regulators could require long-term purchase contracts for RECs as part of RPS policies. Also the structure of long-term demand confirms RECs as reliable collateral assets if utilities need to buy RECs or bundled energy from new projects to supply green pricing programmes and the future retail purchase of RECs from yet-to-be built or yet-to-be completed renewable energy projects.

While emerging market and developing countries might not yet be ready for securitised REC-based funding to support renewable energy, structured finance of electricity commodity (possibly bundled with RECs) could be a feasible temporary arrangement. The concept of RECs includes many characteristics of structured finance. Hence, it could be replicated without the policy and regulatory frameworks for compliance markets based on prescribed RPS policies. Implementation of these policies ultimately leads to the development of common rules and uniform standards for RECs, especially pertaining to the verification of trades.

Like RECs, securitisation of energy monetises the value of future receivables and eliminates the mismatch between generation profile and demand profile vis-à-vis the term of funding requirements. Alternatively, emerging market countries could be invited to join established frameworks of renewable energy trading prior to adopting their own renewable energy strategy, which could form a basis for locally sponsored REC-based securitisation. Structured finance for renewable energy is also useful against the background of rising energy demand in emerging market countries and the importance of more transparent organisation and management of energy supply across national borders.

The securitisation of energy or similar schemes could also be implemented along with energy efficiency projects (e.g., the 2003 World Bank sponsored Uruguay Energy Project) in the effort to decrease developing countries' reliance on imported fuel and reduce their cost of energy in producing goods and services. Conservation and energy efficiency measures targeted to energy efficiency particularly benefit low-income households, especially in combination with energy assistance.

Securitisation of Proceeds from Education

Structured finance could also improve educational systems in emerging market and developing countries. In May 2003, Universidad Diego Portales, a leading private university in Chile, completed the first-ever securitisation of student tuition payments to finance expansion and modernisation. As part of the innovative financing solution of anticipated infrastructure needs, IFC partially guaranteed an eight-year USD 23 million (equivalent in Chile's CPI inflation-based unit of account) bond secured by the university's future tuition flows.[28] This transaction

[28] The transaction was placed mainly with domestic institutional investors including pension funds, insurance companies, and mutual funds. Thus, this transaction contributed to

structure is a demonstration model for replication where certain conditions apply. These include regulatory and legal frameworks that are sufficiently developed, financial constraints of educational institutions that cannot be met by transfer payments from government sources, and the availability of existing or future assets or cash flows that project a profitable investment proposition.[29]

Other Asset Classes

Commodity-exporting emerging market countries may have no immediate need of structured finance due to their accumulation of foreign exchange reserves from energy revenues. However, securitised infrastructural development can diversify revenues away from the energy sector. In addition, in countries with capital account restrictions, central banks could issue securitised debt in order to sterilise capital inflows, which it manages in a foreign investment portfolio.

Conclusion

A handful of more advanced emerging market countries have incubated nascent local securitisation markets. But securitisation is still virtually absent in countries where development finance is needed most and where capital markets have not graduated to a level of maturity that can sustain securitised issuance. With a solid macroeconomic situation, greater fiscal consolidation, and significant structural reforms, this is bound to change in light of buoyant capital flows to emerging markets. Although large-scale indirect securitisation still leads the way, locally sponsored structured finance is following closely behind. Eventually, understanding the extent to which structured finance can benefit local capital market development and accompanying social-economic advancement will reign supreme.

The positive market response to structured finance in emerging markets is encouraging at a time when securitization on conventional asset classes remains largely dormant. First green shoots of structured microfinance and infrastructure speak well of the compelling proposition of securitisation to deliver profitably on development objectives. Given the existing intensity of investor interest in emerging market assets, the potential of securitisation is considerable, especially as more

the development of local capital markets and the availability of local currency financing options.

[29] Governments in other emerging market regions, especially in Asia, have also recognized the benefits of directly securitizing government revenues. In February 2000, the Task Force on Infrastructure of India's *Planning Commission* approved a proposal to securitise a tax surcharge called *cess* for the use of the country's road networks on petrol and diesel in order to finance infrastructure projects. The cess is an additional tax above the normal rates of direct and indirect taxes. Since all income taxes in India are subject to a two percent education cess (applicable on the total tax paid), securitising these receivables and directing them to educational institutions would represent a natural extension of the securitisation market.

and more opportunities from financial innovation beckon. However, these will be unlocked only by joint efforts between private and concessional creditors, such as international and development banks, together with far-reaching public-sector initiatives.

References

Ali, P.U. (2007): "Eco-Finance and Securitization: Carbon as a New Asset Class," in: de Vries-Robbe, J.J. and P.U. Ali (eds.) Innovations in Securitization Yearbook 2007, pp. 97–105.

Aulisi, A.; Hanson, C. (2004): "Developing 'New Generation' Green Power Products for Corporate Markets in North America," World Resource Institute, Washington, DC (December).

Borod, R.S.; Tan, M. (2006): "Carbon: Is it Hot or is it a New Asset Class?" International Securitization and Finance Report (February 15).

Byström, H. (2007): "Structured Microfinance," Journal of Structured Finance 13(2), 26–28.

Chavee, X.; Kochubka, G.; Eddy, J. (2007): "MFI Rating Methodology," RatingsDirect, Standard & Poor's (19 June).

EU Directive (2001): "2001/77/EC of the European Parliament and of the Council of 27 September 2007 on the Promotion of Electricity Produced from Renewable Energy Sources in the Internal Eletricity Market," Official Journal L, 283, 33–40 (27 October).

Fox, S.; Gil, J.P.; Kabance, G.; Valdés, J.C. (2007): "Rating Methodology for Bolivian Microfinance Credits," Criteria Report, Structured Finance, Fitch Ratings (April 19).

Goswami, M.; Jobst, A.; Long, X. (2009): "An Investigation of Some Macro-Financial Linkages of Securitization," IMF Working Paper 9/26 (International Monetary Fund, Washington, D.C.).

Harford, T. (2005): The Undercover Economist: Exposing Why the Rich Are Rich, the Poor Are Poor – and Why You Can Never Buy a Decent Used Car! Oxford University Press, Oxford.

Jobst, A.; Kunzel, P.; Mills, P.; Sy, A. (2007): "Shari'ah-Compliant Securities – Islamic Finance Expanding Rapidly," IMF Survey Magazine, International Monetary Fund (19 September).

Jobst, A. (2010): "Managed Collateralized Debt Obligations (CDOs)," in: Cont, R. (ed.) Encyclopedia of Quantitative Finance (Chichester, UK: John Wiley & Sons Ltd.), pp. 1113–1115.

Jobst, A. (2007): "The Economics of Islamic Finance and Securitization," Journal of Structured Finance 13(1) (Spring), 1–22. Also published as IMF Working Paper 07/117 (May).

Jobst, A. (2007): "Public Sector Securitization in Emerging Markets", in: de Vries-Robbe, J.J. and P.U. Ali (eds.) Innovations in Securitization Yearbook 2007, pp. 407–428.

Jobst, A. (2006): "Sovereign Securitization in Emerging Markets," Journal of Structured Finance 12(3) (Winter), 2–13.

Jobst, A. (2005): "Need for Vigilance by CDO Investors," Financial Times, Comments & Letters (4 November).

Ketkar, S.; Ratha, D. (2004–2005): "Recent Advances in Future-Flow Securitization," The Financier 11/12.

Kota, I. (2007): "Microfinance: Banking for the Poor," Back to Basics, Financial and Development (June), International Monetary Fund (IMF), Washington, D.C., pp. 44f.

Wardle, S. (2005): "Helping the Poor via the Capital Markets: Economic Development Deals New Street Sector," Investment Dealer's Digest (February).

Wilson, R. (2004): "Overview of the Sukuk Market," in: Adam, N.J. and A. Thomas (eds.) Islamic Bonds: Your Guide to Issuing, Structuring and Investing in Sukuk. Euromoney Books, London.

CHAPTER 7

Shari'ah Compliant Structured Finance – Characteristics, Analogies and Legal Risks in Common Law Jurisdictions

Paul U. Ali[*]

Islamic finance, in the manner in which it is executed today, represents the use of conventional financial instruments to raise funds in a manner consistent with the precepts of Islamic law or *Shari'ah*. Of those precepts, perhaps the most important, from a financing perspective, is the prohibition of unlawful profits as exemplified by interest ('riba') and gains from speculation or trading in risk ('gharar'). This prohibition means that fund-raising transactions whose legal 'form' – and that term is used here deliberately – is that of a loan or other interest-based instrument have no place within the Islamic finance universe.

In this sense, Islamic finance is analogous to another type of ethically-informed financing, namely socially responsible investment ('SRI'). Both Islamic finance and SRI are concerned with objectives in addition to the exclusively economic objectives of sourcing funds and delivering returns, and both impose strictures on how those goals may be achieved. Islamic finance requires the *"parties to a transaction to be just, fair and ethical in their dealings with one another"*[1] and, due to the risk-sharing entailed by that requirement under Islamic law, prohibits the provider of funds from charging interest to the recipient of the funds. Similarly, SRI introduces an ethical overlay to the investment of funds by, for instance, prohibiting funds from being invested in what are considered to be unethical industries (the armaments, alcohol, gambling, nuclear energy, pornography and tobacco industries are prime examples). The common ground between Islamic finance and SRI means that one can readily create an investment fund that complies with Islamic law by modifying the investment criteria of an SRI fund.[2]

However, the modification of investment criteria or the criteria on which funds are provided does not, of itself, wholly account for how Islamic finance deals with

---

* Associate Professor, Melbourne Law School.

1 See Hussain, M. (2008), "A General Introduction to Islamic Finance" in R. Ali (ed), Islamic Finance. Globe Law and Business, London.

2 See Mian, K.M.A. (2008), " Sharia Screening and Islamic Equity Indexes " in R. Ali (ed), Islamic Finance, page 26–27. Globe Law and Business, London.

the exclusion of interest-based instruments. For that one must turn to structured finance. Unlike SRI, structured finance is not inherently ethically-informed. Yet – when added to SRI – it enables a clearer picture of Islamic finance to emerge. One can use SRI to explain, by way of analogy, the basis on which funds are made available in Islamic finance; for instance, the provision of funds to businesses that produce or distribute alcohol, pornography or pork would violate Islamic law.[3]

Many contemporary Islamic financing transactions have been devised by modifying the elements of conventional structured finance to conform to the precepts of Islamic law. Thus, to the extent that Islamic finance is transacted in jurisdictions (such as England, Malaysia and Singapore, all of which are important centres for Islamic finance) whose laws are not exclusively Islamic in nature, the precepts of Islamic law that inform Islamic finance can be depicted as an additional set of parameters within which an Islamic finance-transaction must operate. A key parameter is prohibition on interest. In the above jurisdictions, this is not a legal rule in the sense that non-compliance does not render the transaction illegal, but it does render the transaction un-Islamic and, by so doing, destroys the very rationale for the transaction.

The substitution of one instrument for another where the two instruments have different legal forms but have the same substantive or economic function is a matter with which structured finance has long been familiar. Indeed, at the heart of structured finance is the elevation of legal form over economic substance, namely crafting the legal form of a transaction so as to deliver the optimal mix of accounting, taxation and regulatory capital treatment for that transaction. This is nowhere better illustrated than by the development of Islamic securitisation or '*Sukuk*' transactions.[4]

Islamic finance, like structured finance, can thus be depicted as a form of legal arbitrage where a non-interest-based instrument is used in place of an interest-based instrument to ensure compliance with the parameters within which Islamic finance must operate. The substantive equivalence of the two instruments, however, means that the way in which investors evaluate potential investments is not disturbed: the returns on an Islamic law-compliant instrument can be benchmarked against the returns on a conventional instrument as can the putative diversification benefits of the two instruments.

For investors as well as end-users this potentially is a 'best of both worlds' solution. It allows Muslim investors to obtain returns, and Muslim end-users to obtain funds, via transactions that are *Shari'ah*-compliant and offers new investment opportunities for other investors as well as enabling other end-users to diversify their funding sources. Moreover, for emerging markets with sizeable Muslim

[3] See Mian, K.M.A. (2008), " Sharia Screening and Islamic Equity Indexes " in R. Ali (ed), Islamic Finance, page 27. Globe Law and Business, London.

[4] See Box, T. and M. Asaria (2005), "Shariah, Sukuk and Securitisation" in J.J. de Vries Robbé and P.U. Ali (eds), Securitisation of Derivatives and Alternative Asset Classes, pp. 367–370. Kluwer Law International, The Hague.

populations, Islamic finance provides an acceptable means for enhancing the finance sector and enabling greater access to finance. It also – due to its similarity with SRI – represents an acceptable means of promoting development and environmental goals in those markets.

There, however, is one major legal risk involved in the use of Islamic finance. Compliance with the precepts of Islamic law does not mean that a transaction is free from legal risk. The legal risk is one to which structured finance – given its predilection for form over substance – is particularly susceptible; this is the risk that a court or regulator will disregard the form of the transaction and instead treat the transaction as if it took some other form on the basis that that latter form better accords with the substance of the transaction.

In the case of Islamic finance, this could well mean that the transaction is recast in a form that conflicts with Islamic law, resulting in a legal (according to the laws of the jurisdiction) but un-Islamic and thus pointless transaction.

Types of Shari'ah Compliant Financing

The substitution of non-interest-based instruments for loans in Islamic finance often takes two forms:[5]

Murabaha

The acquisition of an asset is financed via the substitution of a sale plus an on-sale for a loan plus a sale.[6] In the case of the latter, the financier makes a loan to its customer which the customer then uses to purchase the asset. In contrast, in the case of a *murabaha*, the financier purchases the asset and on-sells that asset to the customer. The customer is typically obligated to pay the purchase price (which includes a margin above the price paid by the financier) in installments.

Ijara

An *ijara* is a lease[7]. Where a customer is seeking to utilise its own property to raise funds, an *ijara* structured as a sale and lease-back is often used.[8] This is essentially

---

5 Two other transactions are commonly encountered in Islamic finance, *mudarabah* and *musharaka*; but, as these are a type of partnership or joint venture and thus resemble conventional equity financing, they are not considered in the context of the discussion of legal risk in this chapter.

6 See Vogel, F.E. and S.L. Hayes (1998), Islamic Law and Finance: Religion, Risk and Return, pp. 140–143. Kluwer Law International, The Hague.

7 See Vogel, F.E. and S.L. Hayes (1998), Islamic Law and Finance: Religion, Risk and Return, pp. 143–145. Kluwer Law International, The Hague.

8 See Ayub, M. (2007), Understanding Islamic Finance, p. 295. John Wiley & Sons: Chichester.

no different to a conventional sale and lease-back. The customer sells an asset to the financier and receives from the financier the purchase price for that asset. The asset is then leased by the financier back to the purchaser, and the rentals which are to be paid by the purchaser to the financier during the term of the lease equate to the purchase price paid by the financier plus interest.[9]

The first of these examples has obvious similarities to a loan, especially where the financier's margin is expressed as a percentage of the purchase price[10] or an interest rate is used as the benchmark for calculating the margin[11] and where the sale agreement between the financier and the customer contains terms more commonly found in loan agreements than in conventional sale agreements (such as acceleration and the imposition of a penalty amount on the occurrence of an event of default).[12] The legal risk – aside from issues of compliance with Islamic law – is whether a court or regulator would treat this sale as a loan. The customer could be said to owe a debt to the financier (the (marked-up) purchase price or principal plus interest) and, to the extent that a *murabaha* involves the grant of a security interest, that security interest is taken over assets other than the asset being financed.[13] The more complex case of legal risk as it applies to the *ijara* example is dealt with in the next section of this chapter.

Legal Risks for Shari'ah Compliant Transactions in Common Law Jurisdictions

The key point to note when considering the efficacy of Islamic law-compliant financing transactions is that, in many of the jurisdictions where those transactions are executed, the law of that market is not exclusively governed by Islamic law. Accordingly, while the utility of the transaction depends upon compliance with Islamic law (in terms of achieving the objectives of the transaction, including attracting Muslim investors), the legal treatment of that transaction will depend on a system of law outside the ambit of Islamic law – and, importantly, in contrast to Islamic law, that system is likely to uphold interest and recognise loans and other interest-based transactions. This is the same risk as that which confronts conven-

---

9 See Calnan, R. (2006), Taking Security: Law and Practice, p. 165. Jordans, Bristol.

10 See Box, T. and M. Asaria (2005), "Shariah, Sukuk and Securitisation" in J.J. de Vries Robbé and P.U. Ali (eds), Securitisation of Derivatives and Alternative Asset Classes, p. 364. Kluwer Law International, The Hague.

11 See Usmani, M.T. (2002) An Introduction to Islamic Finance, pp. 48–49. Kluwer Law International, The Hague.

12 See Khan, B.A. and A.R. Al Shaikh (2008), "Application of Islamic Finance to Trade Finance" in R. Ali (ed), Islamic Finance, pp. 87–87. Globe Law and Business, London.

13 See Box, T. and M. Asaria (2005), "Shariah, Sukuk and Securitisation" in J.J. de Vries Robbé and P.U. Ali (eds), Securitisation of Derivatives and Alternative Asset Classes, p. 364. Kluwer Law International, The Hague.

tional structured finance transactions, namely the risk that an Islamic financing transaction will be viewed as involving a secured loan masquerading as a sale. As will be seen below, from the discussion of the *ijara*, there are two aspects to this risk (and these comments also apply to the *murabaha*): first, that the sale element of the transaction, if it does not constitute an absolute transfer of the subject matter of the sale, will instead be treated as a transfer by way of security, leading to the entire transaction being treated as a secured loan; and, second, that the economic substance of the transaction as a whole is that of a secured loan rather than a sale and, consequently, the transaction should be treated as the former, not the latter.

Islamic finance is thus, in those markets, vulnerable to a legally adverse treatment of the instruments (including sales and leases) used to achieve *Shari'ah*-compliance.

The *ijara* transaction mentioned above provides a clear example of this. It is a common standalone substitute for a conventional secured loan. It also constitutes one of the most important asset classes for Islamic securitisation or *Sukuk* transactions.[14] Were *ijara* transactions to be legally characterised as secured loans that would very likely arrest the development of the Islamic securitisation market.

Sale and lease-back transactions have the same economic substance as secured loans. For an *ijara*, it is as if the customer – rather than selling its asset to the financier and leasing that asset back from the financier – had, instead, granted a security interest over the asset to the financier to secure the repayment of the loan (represented by the purchase price paid by the financier). The courts, in common law jurisdictions (several of which are important centres for Islamic finance), have usually been reluctant to characterise sale and lease-back transactions as secured loans, simply because of the common economic substance of the two classes of transactions.[15]

The precedence accorded to the legal form of a transaction over its economic substance has perhaps as its high water-mark the decision in the Australian case of *Beconwood Securities Pty Ltd v ANZ Banking Group Ltd.*[16] The court in that case stated that the proper characterisation of a transaction (a securities loan rather than a sale and lease-back) was to be "determined by its legal nature, not to its economic effect" with the legal nature to be ascertained from the terms in which the transaction had been documented and "the genesis of the transaction, its background, its context, and the market in which the parties are operating". This opinion that the matter of characterisation is predominantly one of construction is, however, at odds with the views recently expressed by the highest courts in England where

---

14 See Usmani, M.T. (2002) An Introduction to Islamic Finance, pp. 80–81 Kluwer Law International, The Hague; Aquil, B. and I. Mufti (2008), "Innovation in the Global Sukuk Market and Legal Structuring Considerations", pp. 104–106 in R. Ali (ed), Islamic Finance. Globe Law and Business, London; Testa, D. (2008), "Fixed Income Sukuk: Prospects for Corporate Issuance", pp. 118–119, in R. Ali (ed), Islamic Finance. Globe Law and Business, London.

15 See Calnan, R. (2006), Taking Security: Law and Practice, p. 166. Jordans, Bristol.

16 Federal Court of Australia, 2 May 2008.

considerably greater weight has been given to the economic substance of the transaction; and where the courts have expressed their willingness to look beyond the terms of the transaction to its economic substance and recast those terms in a manner more consistent with that substance.[17]

In determining whether a sale and lease-back should more properly be considered a secured loan, the courts in common law jurisdictions have typically accorded weight to factors such as the following:[18]

- Whether the customer has the right to buy back the asset on maturity of the lease and, if so, whether the stipulated purchase price is a nominal amount. The presence of a buy-back right, particularly at a nominal amount (taking account of the second factor below), indicates the right of the customer to redeem the asset *in specie* and that right of redemption is critical in distinguishing a secured loan from a sale or lease;
- Whether the aggregate value of the rental payments to be made by the customer during the term of the lease covers or exceeds the purchase price paid by the financier for the asset. The obligation on the part of the customer to pay a total amount (taking into account any residual payment that must be paid to buy back the asset) in excess of the purchase price is indicative of an amount that includes an interest component (especially if the so-called rental payments have been calculated by reference to a benchmark interest rate);
- Whether the financier or the customer bears all of the risks and benefits associated with the asset. If the customer, not the financier, assumes the burdens associated with ownership of the asset (such as the risk of a deterioration in the value of the asset below the amount that the customer is obligated to pay the financier, and the obligation to pay of insurance and taxes) or has the benefit of any residual value in the asset beyond what the customer is obligated to pay the financier, that indicates that the sale limb of the sale and lease-back is less than an absolute transfer of ownership to the financier and is, instead, a transfer by way of security; and
- Whether the term of the lease covers the useful life of the asset. A sale and lease-back for or close to the useful life of the asset indicates that the sale limb is in fact a sale rather than a transfer by way of security.

---

[17] See Neagle, A.M. (2008), "Recharacterization Risk in Securitization and Other Structured Finance Transactions – Looking Beyond the Demise of the Fixed Charge", pp. 349–360 in J.J. de Vries Robbé and P.U. Ali (eds), Expansion and Diversification of Securitization. Kluwer Law International, The Hague.

[18] See Brown, N. and M. Newbury (1990), "Lessons for Sale and Leaseback Transactions", Journal of International Banking Law 5(5), 209–212 as well as Oei, S.Y. (2008), "Context Matters: The Recharacterization of Leases in Bankruptcy and Tax Law", American Bankruptcy Law Journal, Vol. 82, 635–692.

An *ijara* that has been structured as a sale and lease-back typically displays the above factors, leading to the real risk that a court or regulator might choose to treat the *ijara* as an in-substance secured loan – a treatment that would render the transaction un-Islamic and thus of nil value for the purposes for which it has been executed due to the transaction's contravention of the prohibition against riba.

Conclusion

This brief paper seeks to place Islamic finance within the legal context of the particular market in which such a transaction has been executed. The structuring of a successful Islamic finance transaction requires not only compliance with the precepts of Islamic law but also confidence as to how that transaction will be viewed by the non-Islamic laws of the relevant market. The *ijara* – which is one of the vital elements of Islamic securitisation – well demonstrates this quandary. The re-characterisation of an *ijara* as a secured loan defeats the purpose for which the *ijara* has been selected, namely to provide funds to the customer and deliver returns to the financier, or the investors in a *Sukuk* transaction backed by the *ijara*, in a manner consistent with the precepts of Islamic law.

Moreover, the precedence of legal form over economic substance on which much of Islamic finance (and structured finance generally) is predicated requires a degree of judicial or regulatory tolerance or accommodation, something that may be less in evidence in the current economic environment. The hostility with which credit default swaps are now being viewed is a stark lesson in how changes in the economic environment can affect the legal treatment of financial instruments. The changes in regulatory attitudes to credit derivatives are well illustrated by the release in July 2009 by the US National Conference of Insurance Legislators of its "Credit Default Insurance Model Legislation" which treats covered credit default swaps as insurance. Similar initiatives have also been proposed by the States of Missouri and Virginia.[19]

However, Islamic finance can offer emerging markets with sizeable Muslim populations a useful means of expanding the availability of finance and enhancing the financial infrastructure of those markets in a manner that meets the religious aspirations of the local population. For the same reasons, Islamic finance is capable of being harnessed to achieve development or environmental objectives in those emerging markets. In addition, any disparity between the treatment of a financial instrument under Islamic law and how that instrument might be viewed within the broader legal framework of the jurisdiction in which that instrument is executed can readily be addressed via legislation.

[19] In November 2008 and January 2009 respectively.

References

Aquil, B.; Mufti, I. (2008): "Innovation in the Global Sukuk Market and Legal Structuring Considerations" in R. Ali (ed), Islamic Finance. Globe Law and Business, London.

Ayub, M. (2007): Understanding Islamic Finance. John Wiley & Sons: Chichester.

Box, T.; Asaria, M. (2005): "Shari'ah, Sukuk and Securitisation" in J.J. de Vries Robbé and P.U. Ali (eds), Securitisation of Derivatives and Alternative Asset Classes. Kluwer Law International, The Hague.

Brown, N.; Newbury, M. (1990): "Lessons for Sale and Leaseback Transactions", Journal of International Banking Law 5(5), 209–212.

Calnan, R. (2006): Taking Security: Law and Practice. Jordans, Bristol.

Hussain, M. (2008): "A General Introduction to Islamic Finance" in R. Ali (ed), Islamic Finance. Globe Law and Business, London.

Khan, B.A.; Al Shaikh, A.R. (2008): "Application of Islamic Finance to Trade Finance" in: Ali, R. (ed), Islamic Finance. Globe Law and Business, London.

Mian, K.M.A. (2008): "Shari'ah Screening and Islamic Equity Indexes" in: R. Ali (ed), Islamic Finance. Globe Law and Business, London.

Neagle, A.M. (2008): "Recharacterization Risk in Securitization and Other Structured Finance Transactions – Looking Beyond the Demise of the Fixed Charge" in J.J. de Vries Robbé and P.U. Ali (eds), Expansion and Diversification of Securitization. Kluwer Law International, The Hague.

Oei, S.Y. (2008): "Context Matters: The Recharacterization of Leases in Bankruptcy and Tax Law", American Bankruptcy Law Journal 82, 635–692.

Testa, D. (2008): "Fixed Income Sukuk: Prospects for Corporate Issuance" in R. Ali (ed), Islamic Finance. Globe Law and Business, London.

Usmani, M.T. (2002): An Introduction to Islamic Finance. Kluwer Law International, The Hague.

Vogel, F.E.; Hayes, S.L. (1998): Islamic Law and Finance: Religion, Risk and Return. Kluwer Law International, The Hague.

CHAPTER 8

Securitization of Worker Remittances

Heather Hughes[*, **]

Introduction

Financial institutions are looking for ways to leverage the value of the cash that emigrant workers send to their home countries. Some banks in developing countries have securitized remittance cash flows for this purpose,[1] but only a portion of remittance securitizations include worker remittances. Likewise, only a handful of scholars have discussed collateralizing debt instruments with worker remittances in particular; most tend to lump worker remittance securitization with future flow securitization in emerging markets generally.

Yet, aid institutions and other non-profits cite remittance-backed bonds as a way to tap the development potential of the money that workers send home.[2] The size and stability of worker remittances have caused a great surge of interest. Worker remittance securitizations present specific instances in which parties in remittance-receiving countries have harnessed the value of this cash flow in order to gain access to capital markets.

---

* Associate Professor, American University, Washington College of Law.

** I want to thank Sam Fox, Fitch Ratings; Gabriel Wieder, Standard & Poor's; Takatoshi Kamezawa, Inter-American Development Bank, and Emil Arca, Dewey & LeBoeuf LLP. Much of my understanding of the remittance securitization market comes from conversations with them.

1 In describing remittance cash flow securitization, this article focuses only on transactions that are rated by an international rating agency. Information on unrated deals is difficult to obtain.

2 For example, see "Ideas, World Commission on the Social Dimension of Globalization, Maximizing Remittances for Development," http://www.ilo.org/dyn/idea/ideasheet.display?p_idea_id=64; Kevin O'Neil, Migration Policy Institute, Summary Report: Discussion on Migration and Development: Using Remittances and Circular Migration as Drivers for Development, at 2 (Apr. 2003), www.migrationpolicy.org/pubs/sandiego-report.doc; Facility for Euro-Mediterranean Investment and Partnership, European Investment Bank, Study on remittances sent by Mediterranean migrants from Europe, www.eib.org/projects/publications/study-on-remittances-sent-by-mediterranean-migrants-from-europe.htm; Ulysses de la Torre, Expat Remittances Bail Out Struggling Banks, IPS Migration Stories, July 8, 2005, http://ipsnews.net/migration/stories/expat.html.

This article discusses remittance securitizations in general and securitizations that involve primarily worker remittances in particular. Given the impact of migration and displacement of workers, and the political capital surrounding the issues of immigration and labor, it is important to consider whether securitization of worker remittances presents a special opportunity to use structured finance to benefit the poor. Worker remittance securitization has the potential to generate better and lower cost services for worker remittance senders and receivers, in addition to providing capital for development. Future flow transactions depend upon an originating bank's capacity to retain or expand its market share of the cash flow it has securitized. Therefore, worker remittance securitizations can, potentially, offer an incentive for banks to encourage remittance senders and receivers to use formal banking systems.

Under certain conditions,[3] remittance securitization can enable banks in developing regions to raise funds at advantageous rates. This chapter explains how remittance securitization works and raises questions about this financing practice.

Is it useful to distinguish worker remittance-based transactions from other future flow securitizations? If so, how might this benefit workers and their communities? Would it be desirable to attempt to draft contracts with provisions that facilitate use of these transactions to benefit worker remittance senders and receivers in new dimensions? Discussion of these questions can deepen understanding of the development potential of remittance securitization.

A Basic Discussion of Remittance Securitization

Remittances include numerous types of transfers such as check payments, wire transfers, and credit card payments. Though any type of remittances may be securitized, remittance securitization refers most commonly to securitization of diversified payment rights. Diversified payment rights are the rights (but not the obligations) that a bank has in the payment orders that it receives to pay funds to beneficiaries.

For example, if a bank in Latin America receives wire transfers of funds sent by workers in the U.S. to relatives near the bank, the bank's rights to receive these funds (but not its obligation to pay the funds to the relatives) are diversified payment rights. Securitizing remittances turns on the fact that a bank's receipt of a remittance is separate from its obligation to pay the party to whom the remittance was sent.

---

[3] Remittance securitization is advantageous when, among other things, a country's risk profile causes banks to seek financing on rates that are better than local sovereign rates. For more discussion on this, see Gabriel Wieder, Gary Kochubka, and Diane Audino, Why is Future Flow Issuance Flowing in Turkey But Ebbing in Latin America? Standard & Poor's, November 6, 2006 (hereinafter "S&P Report 2006").

In a nutshell, securitization is the sale of assets to a special purpose vehicle or "SPV" that then incurs debt secured by the assets. For purposes of securitization, a key feature of remittances is that they are a type of future cash flow – a stream of cash generated by the ongoing business of the bank. In a future flow securitization, a bank seeking to raise funds sells the first right to receive a particular future income stream to an SPV that is incorporated and located offshore. The SPV then issues debt instruments that are collateralized by the future income stream. The SPV passes the proceeds of the issuance through to the bank as consideration for the first right to receive the cash flow.

The bank seeking to raise capital is the "originator" or the "originating bank." The SPV is the "issuer" of the debt instruments. The parties that purchase the debt instruments from the SPV are the "investors."

Pursuant to agreements among the originating bank and the various institutions (such as correspondent banks) through which it receives funds from abroad, these institutions direct the securitized cash flow to an offshore account managed by a trustee. The trustee collects the receivables and makes the principal and interest payments to investors.

For example, in the case of securitization of worker remittances, the originating bank sells to an SPV the first right to receive funds that migrant workers remit (pay in for transfer). Cash from remittances builds up in the account maintained by the trustee until the next payment of principal and interest is owed to the investors. After the trustee pays the investors, it passes the excess cash through to the originating bank.

If there is an event of default on the debt instruments, all of the cash held in the collection account at that point is captured by the investors to be applied to the outstanding debt. This would not in any way absolve the originating bank of the obligation to pay the parties to whom remittances were sent. But the bank would not be able to satisfy that obligation out of the remittance funds that were received by the trustee in the offshore account at the time of default.

A default could result in an originating bank in a developing region being unable to make cash available to recipients of remittances. The bank would probably seek to avoid this result by satisfying its obligation to disburse the money to its intended recipient from any cash the bank could secure for that purpose. If the bank were not in a position to do this, then the risk associated with remittance securitization could bear directly upon individual remittance receivers.

Note that remittance receivers bear similar risk whenever remittances are sent, as a bank could default or go into bankruptcy before these receivers retrieve funds. A remittance securitization could possibly exacerbate difficulties in attempting to recover remitted funds, because the funds are in the hands of the offshore trustee. However, it seems that remittance securitization would not have effects on a bank in default that differ materially from the effects of any other type of securitization to which the bank could be a party.

In any event, rating agencies and practitioners note that remittance-backed bonds tend to perform well. This is in part due to high coverage levels, i.e. issuances represent only a portion of future remittance flows so that reduced flows cannot easily jeopardize the transaction.[4]

Some remittance securitizations primarily consist of worker remittances; others have involved a range of types of remittances of which emigrant workers' monies make up only a small percentage. For example, a 1999 issuance by Banco Cuscatlán in El Salvador and a 2001 issuance by Banco do Brasil were driven mainly by worker remittances. In contrast, in a 2001 issuance by Banco de Crédito del Perú, worker remittances comprised a small percentage of the securitized payment rights, in the range of about ten percent. Eight remittance securitizations in Brazil in 2008 have not been driven by worker remittances.

Emil Arca of Dewey & LeBoeuf reports that there has not been much securitization activity (in 2008 and 2009) involving individual remittance flows, but that this does not indicate that the practice is declining.[5] Programs are still in place in areas where future flow securitizations are largely worker-remittance backed. Arca also indicates that in recent reports worker remittances are projected to decline for the first time but this should not affect worker-remittance backed securitizations. Coverage levels in these transactions are sufficiently high that even if individual remittance flows decrease, remittance-backed debt instruments should continue to perform well.

The credit enhancement associated with future flow securitization stems from factors different from those associated with existing asset securitization. In an existing asset deal, credit enhancement stems from the transfer of the securitized assets to the SPV. Such a transfer is designed to isolate the assets from the liabilities of the originator. A remittance securitization with an offshore SPV, on the other hand, is structured to enable originators to achieve a rating that is better than the sovereign rating of the country in which the originating bank operates. The investors' primary concern in a future flow securitization is not whether the SPV is bankruptcy remote, but the strength of the originator as a going concern (and hence the probable size and stability of the future flow of cash being securitized).

The structure of the remittance securitization – the location of the SPV offshore and the sale to the SPV of the right to receive the future cash flow – functions to isolate the future flow from credit risks associated with the originator's jurisdiction, including currency risks and costs, and political risk. Political risk includes the possibilities of a sovereign order to redirect the cash flow or sovereign restrictions on transfer and convertibility of currency. In general, political risk is the risk that a sovereign will take an action that affects the debtor's payment on the debt

4 See Eric Gretch, Gary Kochubka, Gabriel Wieder, Juan Pablo De Mollein, Rosario Buenda, Scenario Analysis: Emerging Market Financial Future Flow Securitizations Should Weather Upsets, Both at Home and Abroad, Standard & Poor's, August 5, 2008 (hereinafter, "S&P Report 2008"); Gregory Kabance, Samuel Fox, Mark Salgado, Back to the Future: Are Emerging Market Future Flows Making a Comeback? Fitch Ratings, July 31, 2008 (hereinafter "Fitch Report 2008").

5 Emil Arca, How to Think About Bankruptcy Risk in Cross-Border Future Flow Transactions After the Avianca Case, The Journal of Structured Finance, (Winter 2005).

instruments. Some would divide the concept of political risk into a) risk of a deliberate act of interference by a sovereign, and b) risk of sovereign acts that, while not aimed at interfering with business transactions, have the effect of interfering with a debtor's ability or willingness to pay.

Note that while remittance securitization minimizes political risks associated with the originating bank's jurisdiction, it also involves offshore political risk. Changes in government policies in remittance senders' jurisdictions can affect remittance flows as well. For example, banks in Latin America that securitize worker remittances would be affected by a change in U.S. policy regarding taxation of worker remittances or immigration and labor. While not likely, such a change could undermine the capacity of developing region originators to service remittance-backed bonds.

In theory, once the future cash flow is sold to the SPV, only the investors who purchased the SPV's bonds have any rights pertaining to it. Practitioners report that laws in many developing countries permit counsel for the originator to opine that the securitized assets have been transferred to the SPV in a true sale transaction and that the remittances would continue to flow through the collection account to service the debt instruments, even if the originator were to become bankrupt.

However, the true sale opinion serves a different purpose in a remittance securitization than in an asset securitization. The purpose of this opinion in the future flow deal is to establish that under the laws of the originator's jurisdiction the transfer of the first right to receive remittances effected a sale to a foreign purchaser. The goal is to minimize political risk, not to isolate the assets from those of the originator such that a U.S. court would find the assets to be unreachable by the originator's creditors. Again, because the securitization is of future flows and not existing assets, the strength of the originator as a going concern is the focus of the ratings analysis, not the isolation of the future flow from the liabilities of the originator.

Securitizations lower costs of capital for originators, but they involve substantial transaction costs. These costs are digestible for the originator if the pool of assets securitized is large enough, and the savings due to credit enhancement are great enough, that the savings in costs of capital outweigh transaction costs.[6]

It appears that a major recent change in the practice of remittance securitization has been the decline in monoline insurance guaranties or wraps for these transactions. Before the financial crisis that began in 2008, debt instruments collateralized by future remittance flows were wrapped – insured by a financial guaranty

6 For example, as Suhas Ketkar and Dilip Ratha of the World Bank explain, if the originator enjoys a 50 basis point savings by borrowing via securitization, a $ 200 million issuance leads to a saving of about $ 5 million over a four-year period and $ 11 million over a seven-year period. This example is not meant to assert that originators in fact can expect 50 basis point savings on securitized deals. It simply presents an example of the concept of lower costs of capital outweighing what appear to be very high transaction costs. Suhas Ketkar and Dilip Ratha, Development Financing During a Crisis: Securitization of Future Receivables, World Bank Policy Research Working Paper No. 2582 (April 2001), hereinafter "Ketkar and Ratha, WPS2582".

from an AAA-rated insurer. These insurers have suffered significant rating downgrades that deplete the value that wraps added to these transactions.

When the future flow securitization market ebbed in 2006 and 2007, practitioners attributed the decline to both a) improved country profiles that have made alternative forms of financing more economical than securitization, and, conversely, b) deteriorating conditions that undermine the capacity of future flow securitizations to provide credit enhancement sufficient to attract the kinds of investors interested in remittance-backed bonds.[7]

As sovereign risk improves, securitization may not be necessary to enable banks to gain access to capital on favorable terms. On the other hand, if sovereign risk deteriorates too much, securitization may not be sufficient to improve the rating of an issuance to the point that it can ensure access to offshore capital markets.

Securitizing future flows from remittances took hold in the mid-1990s. Notably, in January 2001, Banco de Crédito del Perú raised $ 100 million with a bond backed by securitized electronic transfer payment instructions.[8] At that time Banco de Crédito del Perú was receiving close to $ 3 billion annually in electronic transfers,[9] of which worker remittances comprised a relatively small part. The bank arranged with its major correspondent banks (mostly large, U.S. banks such as Bank of America and Bank of New York) for the direction of electronic transfers to an offshore account held in trust by Bank of New York to isolate the payments from Peruvian political risk. The payments were sold to an offshore SPV that issued the debt. MBIA Insurance Rating Corporation, a public insurer, guaranteed timely payment of interest and of principal on maturity.

Commentators note that Banco de Crédito del Perú completed this transaction during a time of political crisis following President Alberto Fujimori's fleeing the country. One often-noted advantage of securitizations of remittances is that they enable developing nation borrowers to access foreign capital even in times of turmoil. The income stream represented by some types of remittances, and, therefore, their value as collateral for debt instruments, can be unaffected by fluctuations in stability that affect sovereign credit and the credit of borrowers in the jurisdiction suffering from volatility.[10]

---

[7] S&P Report 2006.

[8] A remittance-backed bond, 134 Latin Finance 27 (Feb. 2002) (hereinafter "LatinFinance"); United Nations Development Programme, Latin America and Caribbean Sub-Regional Resource Facility, UNDP El Salvador: Worker Remittance as an Instrument for Development, (Dec. 2003) (hereinafter "UNDP El Salvador").

[9] LatinFinance.

[10] In addition to Banco de Crédito del Perú's transaction, other early securitizations of remittance cash flows that attracted attention include a $ 300 million remittance-backed bond issued by Banco National de Mexico in 1998, a November 1999 issuance by Banco Cuscatlán in El Salvador, and a $ 300 million issuance by Banco do Brasil in 2001 (backed by yen remittances from workers in Japan). Banco Cuscatlán's 1999 issuance and this 2001 Banco do Brasil issuance primarily involved worker remittances. UNDP El Salvador.

The Case of Securitization of Worker Remittances

Securitization of worker remittances may present a unique opportunity to use structured finance to benefit the poor. Remittance securitizations are based upon expected future cash flows and depend upon the originating bank's capacity to retain or expand its market share of the securitized cash flow. Therefore, worker remittance securitizations can provide an incentive for banks to encourage remittance senders and receivers to use formal banking systems.

Some large banks have responded to the size and stability of worker remittance flows through programs designed to attract emigrant worker customers. Such efforts include Bank of America's SafeSend program in which migrant workers obtain ATM debit cards that can be used for withdrawals by their relatives in Mexico.[11]

However, numerous reports on remittances have lamented the high cost of sending wages home and the lack of banking services for the poor. This section considers whether and how worker remittance securitization should be distinguished from remittance securitization generally.

Whether or not a securitization is worker remittance-based depends on the nature of the diversified payment rights that a given bank receives and on the issuance and the nature of the collateral involved.

Some researchers have identified a link between remittance securitization and benefits for people sending or receiving remittances. For example, Pedro De Vasconcelos of the Inter-American Development Bank (IDB) reports that remittance securitization offers several potential benefits, including "better and lower cost services for remittances senders and receivers."[12]

Such benefits could have the potential to expand the size of worker remittance cash flows sent through formal banking channels and, therefore, amenable to securitization. If a bank in a developing region were to advertise to remittance-receiving communities that funds received via their correspondent banks would be used to raise capital to benefit the community, wage remitters might respond by using these channels.

However, conveying to emigrant workers and remittance-receiving communities that securitization offers a basis for using one money transfer product or provider over another is a complex task and it is unclear whether originating banks and their correspondent institutions would perceive obstacles in attracting remittance sending and receiving customers.

---

[11] Michael S. Barr, Banking the Poor, 21 Yale Journal on Regulation 121, p. 195 (2004); Carolyn Said, Remittance market draws major players: Banks, cards, credit unions enter the fray, San Francisco Chronicle , July 16, 2006 at F3.

[12] U.N. Department of Economic and Social Affairs, Fourth Coordination Meeting on International Migration, The Multilateral Investment Fund of the Inter-American Development Bank and Remittances, U.N. Doc. UN/POP/MIG-FCM/2005/10 (Oct. 14, 2005) (prepared by Pedro De Vasconcelos).

Securitization of worker remittances is a method of raising capital that can be applied in a range of ways, beneficial to development or not. Investment funds committed to economic development and social responsibility might be interested specifically in worker remittance-backed bonds. Distinguishing worker-remittance based transactions and linking these transactions to lower cost worker-remittance services and investment of proceeds for development could generate a different market for the debt instruments. In order to implement an initiative involving lower cost transfers, the originator and sending institutions would have to enter into agreements regarding the fees or costs to clients associated with various transfers.

Contract provisions in relevant transaction documents could designate proceeds of these transactions for uses associated with development. For example, provisions could require an originator to lower costs or to improve services to wage remitters, or to apply the proceeds of securitization in other ways that benefit remittance-receiving communities.

The identification of specific development objectives and means to secure proper use of funding goes beyond the purpose of this paper. This chapter leaves to others the task of identifying what "development" should mean in this context.

Poverty law scholar Ezra Rosser identifies the surge in interest in worker remittances as part of a larger trend.[13] This trend embraces economic phenomena that imply that the global poor can solve the problem of poverty without sacrifice from wealthier communities, so long as supporting institutions are in place to enable capitalistic self-help. If we take this contention at face value and consider it in relation to securitizations of worker remittances, some issues emerge. For example, it appears that the market for remittance-backed bonds consists in part of conservative, institutional investors that require substantial over-collateralization. Practitioners indicate that remittance-backed bonds tend to out-perform their rating class.[14] If this is the case, are the originators getting the value that they should out of this future cash flow?

This is a complex question to which different actors may have very different approaches. Current investors may insist that originators are maximizing the value of the cash flow, because current levels of collateralization are the minimum levels at which investors will participate. On the other hand, one could argue that investors in remittance-backed bonds should consider having higher risk tolerance regarding these bonds. Bearing higher risk than they do now – without a corresponding increase in profit – could move investors (members of "wealthier communities") towards maximizing proceeds of these transactions in the hands of developing region banks.

To harness more fully the development potential of remittance securitization, it may be useful to identify worker remittance-backed bonds as intimately linked to poverty and migration, marketing them to development-oriented investors with

[13] Ezra Rosser, Immigrant Remittances, 41 Connecticut Law Review 1 (2008).

[14] See Fitch Report 2008.

different standards for collateralization, such as socially conscious or development-oriented investors. Distinguishing securitizations of worker remittances from future flow securitization in emerging markets more generally could facilitate such an effort. Only some worker remittances are sent by or to low income people; in other cases well-compensated professionals send funds to relatives or communities abroad. In many contexts, however, worker remittance cash flows are sent primarily from low income workers to recipients who readily use the support.

If it is worthwhile to distinguish worker remittance-backed transactions from future flow securitization in general, which transactions should be identified – those in which worker remittances make up over ninety percent of the cash flow that is securitized? Or, is some lesser, even minority, percentage enough? Practitioners tend to have a clear idea of which transactions are driven by worker remittances and which by other types of remittances. The question of thresholds of worker remittances involved in any given transaction could arise, if investors, remittance senders and receivers, or originators were to regard these transactions differently given their relationship to migrants and their communities of origin.

References

Arca, Emil (2005): How to Think About Bankruptcy Risk in Cross-Border Future Flow Transactions After the Avianca Case, The Journal of Structured Finance.

Fajnylber, Pablo; Lopez, J. Humberto (2007): Close to Home. In: The Development Impact of Remittances in Latin America (World Bank, Report No. 37026).

Fitch IBCA, Duff & Phelps (2005): Rating Securities Backed by Financial Future Cash Flows.

Fitch Ratings (2006): Future Flow Securitization Ratings Methodology.

Gretch, Eric; Kochubka, Gary; Wieder, Gabriel; De Mollein, Juan Pablo; Buenda, Rosario (2008): Scenario Analysis: Emerging Market Financial Future Flow Securitizations Should Weather Upsets, Both at Home and Abroad, Standard & Poor's.

Jackson, Nathaniel (2006): Inter-American Development. Bank, Securitization of Remittances, www.earth.columbia.edu/cgsd/remittances/documents/Jackson.pdf.

Kabance, Gregory; Fox, Samuel; Salgado, Mark (2008): Back to the Future: Are Emerging Market Future Flows Making a Comeback? Fitch Ratings.

Ketkar, Suhas; Ratha, Dilip (2001): Development Financing During a Crisis: Securitization of Future Receivables, World Bank Policy Research Working Paper No. 2582.

Ketkar, Suhas; Ratha, Dilip (2001): Securitization of Future Flow Receivables: A Useful Tool for Developing Countries, 38 Finance & Development.

Maimbo, Samual Munzele; Ratha, Dilip, eds. (2005): Remittances: Development Impact and Future Prospects.

Patti, James (2005): Presentation: Securitization of Remittances, www.adb.org/Documents/Events/2005/ADB-IADB-MIF-UNDP/jpatti1.pdf.

Rosser, Ezra (2008): Immigrant Remittances, 41 Connecticut Law Review 1.

Standard & Poor's (2004): The Three Building Blocks of an Emerging Markets Future Flow Transaction Rating.

Standard & Poor's (2004): FI Criteria: Bank Survivability Criteria.

Stern, Selma (2005): What Banks Need to Know About Securitization of Future Cash Flows In Emerging Markets, 122 The Banking Law Journal 953.

CHAPTER 9

Structured Finance Approaches to Livelihood Projects in India

Bindu Ananth and Anand Sahasranaman[*]

Introduction

"Livelihood Projects" are projects or activities in critical sectors such as agriculture, microfinance and water that directly impact the well-being and income of low-income households. Entities such as microfinance institutions (MFIs) that make small income generating loans to the rural and urban poor or small/medium enterprises involved in provision of clean drinking water or low-income housing services etc. are examples of institutions involved in the livelihood space.

In India, one of the major challenges facing such entities is a lack of access to capital. Financing these institutions is generally perceived to be highly risky, leading to very little investment in this space. Despite the fact that some of these entities have fundamentally robust businesses in addition to a strong social impact, they are unable to raise the funds to enable them to sustain themselves and scale up.

In this scenario, it becomes imperative for entities in the livelihood space to explore hitherto untapped sources of capital such as capital markets. As long as there is a sound underlying business, appropriate financial instruments can be structured to enable these institutions to access funding from capital markets.

This chapter is organized as follows: The first section deals with the potential role of structured finance in the livelihood sector. Second, the regulatory environment in India is described, before exemplary illustrations of structured solutions in the Indian livelihood sector are provided. Lastly, the role of specialized equity investors is depicted.

Structured Finance and Livelihood

Structured financial instruments fundamentally provide for the transfer of risk using financial engineering techniques such as securitisation. Securitisation involves the issuance of securities backed by a pool of loans or other underlying assets. In

[*] Institute for Financial Management and Research (IFMR) Trust.

the livelihood space, the underlying assets in a securitisation could be microfinance loans, future receivables from water projects, warehouse receipts backed by agricultural commodities etc.

Good financial structuring isolates the various risks involved in a project and allocates them to the parties best equipped to handle them. As the fallout from the recent credit crisis has shown, it is critical that any robust financial structure ensures that all parties in a transaction are incentivised appropriately. In a situation, where all risks in a transaction are passed on to end investors, asset originators and financial intermediaries have little incentive to perform the requisite due diligence at the time of originating and buying asset portfolios.

Another key role for structuring in livelihood projects is to separate debt and equity; essentially to optimize the quantum of equity used. Often, poorly designed projects result in the usage of excessive amounts of equity which hinders scalability.

A typical securitisation involves a number of parties, viz. the originator, the special purpose vehicle (SPV), a rating agency, a trustee and investors.

The use of a bankruptcy-remote SPV allows for delinking the credit risk of the originator from the pool of assets being securitised. The quality of the asset pool being securitised can be further improved through credit enhancements such as guarantees or insurance.

The involvement of a rating agency can help to ascertain the credit quality associated with the portfolio of assets. A strong rating from an agency such as CRISIL in India can provide investors considerable comfort on the fundamental quality of the portfolio of livelihood assets. Rating agencies also constantly monitor portfolio quality, providing a continual check on the assets. As the market for rated assets develops, high quality institutions in the livelihood space will be able

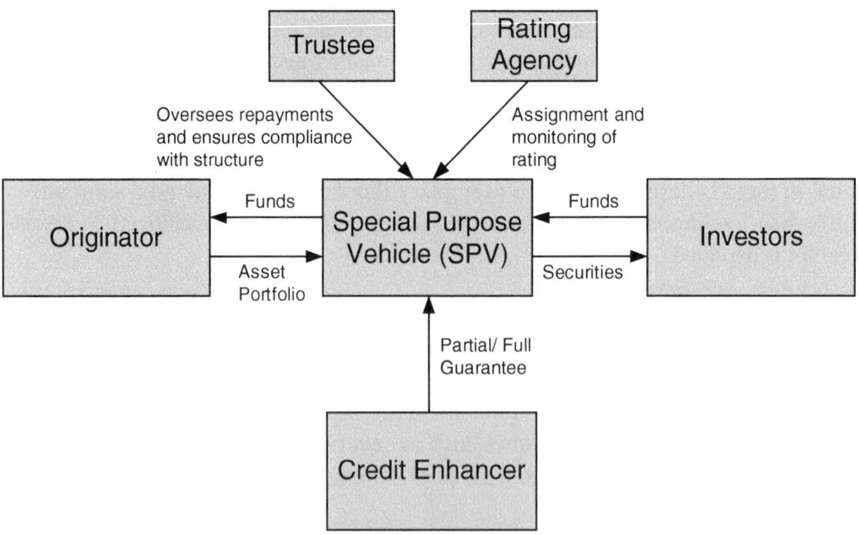

Fig. 1. A typical securitisation structure

to see a more reliable flow of funds throughout the year and also a secular decline in the cost of these funds.

Structuring also opens up possibilities of widening the pool of investors in the livelihood space. Creating rated securities opens up the market to mutual funds and insurance companies, in addition to banks. Also, pooling of assets can be an effective tool of risk diversification for investors. Structuring the liabilities into different tranches of rated notes will serve to attract investors of different risk profiles. The maturity profiles of the securities can also be designed to suit investor requirements.

These new types of assets born through structuring could contribute to creating a deeper and more complete debt market.

Regulatory Scenario in India

The Indian banking regulator, the Reserve Bank of India (RBI), has mandated that 40% of all lending by banks in the country be awarded to the '*Priority Sector*'[1]. RBI broadly defines the Priority Sector as encompassing:

- Agriculture and associated activity such as dairy, fishery, poultry, piggery, bee-keeping etc.
- Small enterprises involved in manufacturing and services
- Retail trade including consumer co-ops and traders dealing in essential commodities
- Microcredit
- Education Loans
- Housing Loans

Of the 40% reserved for all such lending, 18% must be directed towards '*Agriculture*', which involves financing of agriculture activities through direct lending to individual farmers, Self Help Groups (SHGs), and Joint Liability Groups (JLGs).

Most Indian banks have little significant rural penetration and therefore find it difficult to meet this annual requirement. The RBI imposes stringent penalties on any shortfall in respect to this requirement. If a bank finds itself in violation, it can be required to park such shortfall in the Rural Infrastructure Development Fund (RIDF) operated by the National Bank for Agriculture and Rural Development (NABARD) for terms of up to 8 years at very low interest rates. Banks are naturally keen to avoid this, not only because of the cost of parking long term funds at low yields but also because it makes poor strategic sense to be a defaulter in the books of the regulator.

---

[1] See http://www.rbi.org.in/scripts/NotificationUser.aspx?Mode=0&1d=976.

In this scenario, banks would like to invest in high quality agriculture investments. Banks can achieve this by buying securities that, for example, provide exposures to loans made to farmers or warehouse receipts against agricultural produce. But individual MFIs are not able to provide banks access to microloans on the scale they require. Multi-originator securitisations can aggregate portfolios of loans from different MFIs, pool them together and issue securities that qualify as direct agriculture investments as per RBI requirements. Similarly, warehouse receipts issued to farmers can be pooled and securitised, which again could be of great interest to banks. Rating agencies and credit enhancement providers will play very crucial roles in creating a market for such securitised paper.

Illustrations of Structured Solutions in the Livelihood Space

Illustration 1: First Microloan Securitisation in India

Finance in rural India has largely been the domain of Regional Rural Banks and has been aided by the RBI's Priority Sector Lending requirements for all banks. However, the perception of the rural poor as 'bad' credit risks combined with the high costs of rural credit delivery have kept most Indian banks from venturing into rural India. In this scenario, MFIs are seen as having a model that is well suited to the delivery of rural financial services. The group lending models combined with strong credit discipline have resulted in very low historical credit loss rates. Consequently, much of bank finance directed to rural areas has been routed through MFIs. This has been accomplished through a combination of term loans to MFIs and loan portfolio buyouts. However, one tool that can significantly impact MFIs and help them achieve scale to serve more clients is securitisation.

IFMR Capital, an entity promoted by IFMR Trust with the objective of connecting entities that impact low-income households with the capital markets, structured and arranged the first rated securitisation in Indian microfinance in March 2009. The originating institution was Equitas Micro Finance India Pvt. Ltd and the transaction was rated by CRISIL. Two rated tranches of securities were issued by the SPV, the Series A1 tranche subscribed to by a private bank and the A2 tranche purchased by IFMR Capital.

Table 1. First rated securitization in Indian microfinance

Security	*Yield*	*Principal Rs. Million*	*Principal (%)*	*Expected Maturity (Months)*	*Legal Final Maturity (Months)*	*Rating*
Series A1	Fixed	125.4	80%	14	20	AA
Series A2	Residual	31.3	20%	20	20	BBB

This transaction is structured in such a way that the interests of all parties – the originator (Equitas), the structurer and mezzanine finance provider (IFMR Capital) and the senior bank investor – are aligned to incentivise good due diligence and performance of the underlying loan portfolio.

The originator plays a crucial role in servicing the loans, having originated them based on its predefined credit criteria. Now, when the MFI looks to securitise a portfolio of loans, it is essential that it will continue servicing those loans as if they were still on its own balance sheet. These failures in servicing portfolios, coupled with lax underwriting standards of originators were some of the prime reasons that spawned the current credit crisis. In order to ensure high quality of servicing and to signal its confidence on the credit risk of the portfolio, the originator provides the first loss portion of the portfolio. Any losses will first be absorbed by this first loss facility, up to a specified amount.

Financial intermediaries have an important role to play in assessing the quality of the originating MFI. IFMR Capital has come out with a detailed set of underwriting guidelines to assess the quality of the originating MFIs it works with. IFMR Capital performed a comprehensive due diligence on Equitas' processes, systems, financials, management and risk management practices.

An intermediary can establish its credibility by its willingness to take a portion of the risk in the transaction. In the years leading to the credit crisis, large financial intermediaries usually held highly rated super-senior risk. A false sense of security prevailed about the "infallible" nature of this part of the capital structure, however, when defaults accelerated, banks suffered massive market to market losses on account of these positions. Since the intermediary has a crucial role in assessing the quality of the originator and the underlying portfolio, it is ideally incentivized by taking the second loss risk in the structure. The second loss facility or tranche absorbs any losses after the first loss facility is exhausted and will provide additional protection to senior investors.

Through such structuring, the incentives of the originator and intermediary can be aligned with the investor who will hold the senior risk of the portfolio. The investor will be protected from losses to the extent of the first loss facility provided by the originator and second loss facility provided by the financial intermediary.

The credit enhancements in the microloan securitisation transaction were structured keeping these lessons in mind. Equitas provided a first loss facility in the form of cash collateral equal to 11.7% of the principal amount of the portfolio. This cash collateral is used to cover any shortfall in repayments on the AA (so) and BBB (so) securities.

In addition to the above enhancement, the investors in the AA (so) securities are further protected by the junior BBB (so) rated securities held by IFMR Capital, which comprise 20% of the issue size. All payments from the securitised pool will go towards payment of principal and interest on the AA (so) rated Series A1 notes and only when the Series A1 notes have been completely paid off will payments be made to the BBB (so) rated Series A2 notes. The BBB (so) securities are time-subordinated to the AA (so) securities in this structure.

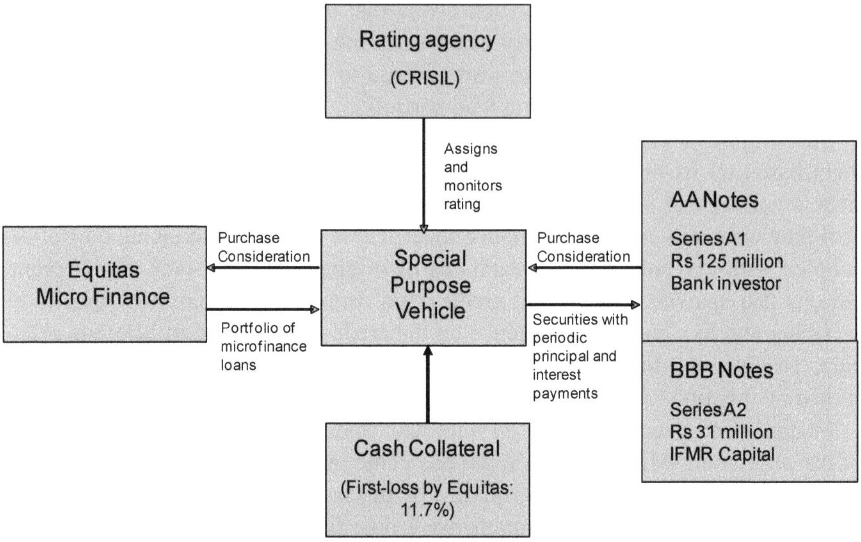

Fig. 2. Rated microloan securitisation structure

These two levels of credit enhancement, provided by the originator and the financial intermediary, ensure that all the parties in the transaction are appropriately incentivised.

Such structured transactions could have a tremendous impact in terms of bringing in a steady supply of debt capital to the microfinance sector. Rated securitisations backed by portfolios of microloans will open up rural finance to investment not only from banks, but also other financial institutions such as mutual funds and insurance companies. This can have a significant impact on lowering MFI's cost of funds and ultimately reducing the cost to the end borrower in rural India.

Illustration 2: A Proposed Structured Project Finance

Structuring can be a powerful tool for project finance. Structured finance techniques can even be used to provide funding mechanisms for entities with limited histories but strong underlying business models and cash flows.

One such possible livelihood securitisation is of a portfolio of clean drinking water plants set up by a servicer company in rural India. The servicer company sells the water from these plants to the local community. To do this, the company gets into long term 8 year agreements with the local government (panchayat) that gives them access to a source of surface water and land to set up the plant. The panchayat owns the plant from day one, having made a down payment of about 20–30% of the capital cost to set up the plant. The remaining is financed through long term loans. Despite the panchayat owning the plant, for the first 8 years the servicing company has the right to collect fees from water sales and use it to cover operating costs and debt service. Any surplus goes into a surplus account, where it stays for 8 years. At the end of 8 years, the surplus is split between the panchayat, the servicer company and the debt provider on a pre-agreed basis.

The company has set up more than 300 plants so far, and is looking to set up more such plants in India. Revenue is generated through water sales on plant location and by delivery. Sales have been augmented through a program of educating people about the benefits of clean drinking water. The plants set up so far have found strong local demand not only for personal and family consumption, but also for livestock. The plants are modular, easy to set up and operations are managed by locals. This is a fundamentally sound business with strong growth prospects.

Structured finance techniques provide a sound avenue for funding such a business. A replicable securitisation structure backed by the revenues generated by water sales can become the basis for sustained debt capital supply to such a business, enabling it to expand and set up more such clean drinking water plants in rural India.

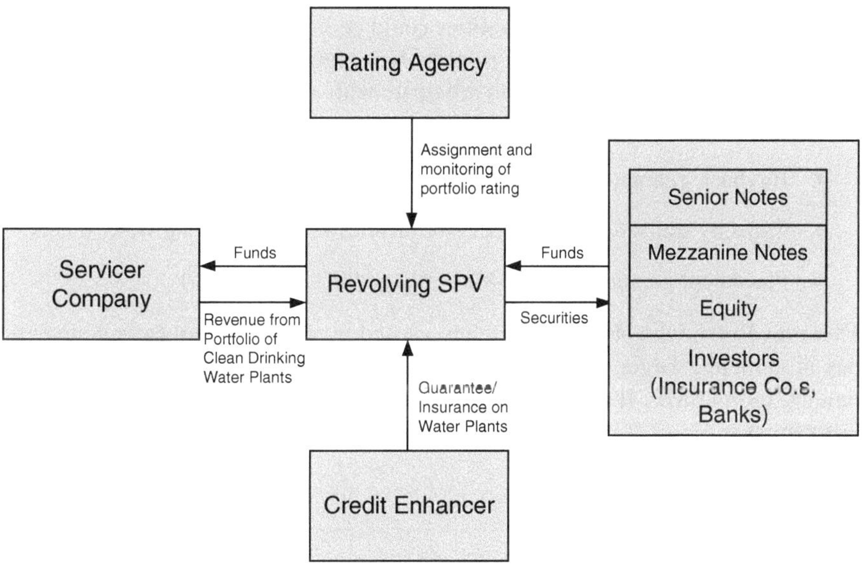

Fig. 3. Potential drinking water plants securitisation structure

The servicer company sells the future revenues generated by water sales from the clean drinking water plants to an SPV, which issues securities backed by these future cash flows. Investors purchase these securities and the funds raised through the issue are used for the construction of the plants. As per the terms agreed, the SPV will pass on the cash flows generated by these plants to the investors.

The rating agency analyses the portfolio of drinking water plants, the servicer company and the sustainability and riskiness of cash flows. Depending on the rating agency's assessment, credit enhancement can be provided in the form of a guarantee or insurance cover on the portfolio of plants.

Given the relatively long payback involved, there is tremendous scope for increasing leverage over time by carefully tracking capacity utilisation at the plant level and, depending on performance trajectory, replacing equity with debt funding.

The long tenor of these rated notes can be of great interest to insurance companies for their investment portfolio.

Creating viable financial structures that enable companies involved in the provision of clean drinking water to access the capital markets will be an important step in making their business plans viable and ultimately help in realising the greater objective of making clean drinking water available to everyone.

Role of Specialised Equity Investors

There is a role for a new class of investors, especially in the context of SMEs, who can creatively participate in risk sharing in entities that are outside the radar of most mainstream investors. Such entities could be in sectors such as food processing, drinking water, skills training, rural tourism, agriculture and dairy.

Specialised equity investors can participate with entities in such sectors via risk sharing mechanisms such as:

- Buyback guarantees (for manufacturing of apparel, foods etc.)
- Capacity utilisation guarantees (for utilities such as drinking water plants)
- Placement guarantees (for SMEs engaged in skill training)

These investors, who absorb uncertainty caused by quantifiable factors, help entities in attracting larger quantities of debt and thereby reduce the overall cost of funding to the SME. IFMR Trust's Network Enterprises Fund is one example of this approach.

Conclusion

Structuring opens up new ways of looking at businesses and assets in the livelihood space. Application of structured finance approaches can lead to the provision of much needed capital market access that could kick-start economic activity in many crucial sectors. Also, the process of creating a structure that works for various stakeholders requires a high level of transparency and therefore serves as an efficient tool for price discovery. Currently, the inefficiency in supply chains has made efficient pricing a difficult proposition. Effective price discovery could go a long way in reducing cost of capital for end borrowers.

CHAPTER 10

The Use of Structured Finance for a Deposit Based MSME Banking Group in Emerging Markets – The Case of ProCredit

*Martin Godemann**

Abstract

ProCredit Holding executed the first "true sale" securitisation of a microfinance loan portfolio in Bulgaria for EUR 47.8 million in 2006. Since then, ProCredit has entered into a number of structured finance transactions representing one of many refinancing options. Structured Finance can be complex in design and create material opportunity costs diverting management resources for a bank. They require investor confidence-building and have no particular advantages or disadvantages in refinancing costs.

Introduction

The ProCredit Holding group consists of 21 financial institutions operating in transition economies and developing countries in Africa, Latin America and Eastern Europe. Its core business is the provision of financial services to very small and small enterprises and households. The loan portfolio is largely financed by retail deposits– the ordinary man or woman living around the corner from our branches. ProCredit offers a range of basic banking products that are demanded by its clientele: loans, guarantees, deposits, domestic and international payments, card services and in some countries e-banking. ProCredit emphasizes staff education in its academies, local training courses and on-the-job-training.

Founded in 1998, ProCredit expanded at a rapid pace. At the end of 2009 it had a loan portfolio of EUR 3.3 billion consisting of 0.9 million loans, deposits of EUR 3 billion held in over 3.8 million customer accounts, and total assets of EUR 4.9 billion. From 2006 to 2008, the average (after-tax) return on equity was close to 12%, and ProCredit remained profitable in 2009. It employs more than 19 000 staff and has a network of over 800 branches.

---

* Manager Group Finance, ProCredit Holding AG.

ProCredit Funding Source Priorities

What has been our strategy to fund our business development? To what extent has funding via capital markets and via structured finance products played a role?

ProCredit's most important source of financing is deposits. This reflects its view that financial institutions issuing loans should largely be funded by deposits, otherwise institutions would either be limited in their growth, and their potential outreach, or will remain overly dependent on volatile capital markets. Funding from IFIs can ease this problem, but not solve it.

There is a lot of talk about private investors, and about mobilising private, i.e. commercial money, as if this was the ultimate litmus test for the viability of a business model, the final blessing for "microfinance". To a certain extent this may be true, as private investors would like their own money to be safely invested while generating an adequate return. However, ProCredit Holding takes a different perspective to "mobilising private money". The primary challenge for ProCredit banks is to create trust with our retail depositors who are our local private and commercial investors. Mobilising these funds is our first litmus test for the viability of our business model and the credibility of our banks in their respective (local) markets. Mobilising these funds is the first "blessing" signaling the professionalism of our banks; only then do international private investors enter the picture.

At the end of 2009, almost 90% of ProCredit's loan portfolio was funded by retail deposits. We do not consider a 90% funding ratio to be sufficient; we aim at a deposit/loan portfolio ratio of well above 100%.

Despite this emphasis on deposit mobilisation, ProCredit Holding sees a crucial role for other sources of funding, including structured finance. As a general strategy, ProCredit aims at having the broadest possible range of financing options available in order to fund the remaining gap between its loan portfolio and its deposit base, to manage its asset-liability-maturity structure and to be able to address any potential liquidity shortage. The non savings financing options currently used by the ProCredit group range from loans from IFIs and commercial banks, to commercial money market lines and overdraft/standby lines, to "plain vanilla" bonds (covered and uncovered, local and international placements, local and international currencies), and finally to structured finance instruments.

ProCredit Activity in Capital Markets

ProCredit began tapping capital markets through relatively small local bond issues placed by our banks in their local markets in Bulgaria and Ukraine. This was followed by various private bond placements by ProCredit Holding AG, the group's parent company, starting in the second half of 2005. In May 2006, in the first true sale securitisation of a microfinance portfolio, ProCredit Bank Bulgaria sold a loan portfolio of EUR 47.8 million. As of end-2007 the outstanding volume of loans sold through this mechanism was close to EUR 100 million. In early 2007,

ProCredit Bank Serbia placed a loan participation note of EUR 125 million with international investors. Other structured finance instruments issued by ProCredit Group include subordinated debt and trust-preferred securities.

ProCredit believes that a sound and logical approach is to begin with straight debt at an early stage of entering these markets, rather than to start with structured finance – especially the securitisation route, as it requires strong institutions.

Launching ProCredit's presence in capital markets with "plain vanilla" issues (in our case, both publicly and privately placed bonds) helped investors to focus on ProCredit and its business and risk profile, rather than on the technicalities of a specific transaction.

Structured finance products, especially securitisation, require substantial management resources. When ProCredit Bank Bulgaria securitised part of its loan portfolio, the bank's senior management had to devote a significant – not to say inordinate –amount of time to the deal due to the tight time frame (four months between kick-off and the funding date) and the structural challenges of the transaction, which was new territory in every respect. It was only thanks to the strong organisational structure of the bank that it was able to handle this challenge while continuing to grow at a rapid pace.

If a structured finance transaction were carried out at an early stage of institutional development, the institution would risk having to allocate too many resources to the project instead of focusing on developing the institution in all its other aspects. Within our group, we have refrained from discussing structured finance solutions with some of our banks which we felt were not ready or which needed to focus on managing other challenges.

Another important aspect is that we see a strong link between the quality of our assets and the quality of our institutions. Using transaction structures such as securitisation as a means of de-linking the institutional risk from the risks of the securitised assets might work as a corporate funding strategy in a mature (Western) market with well-established, well-known, credible market players. In our environment, however, investors first have to be convinced that the institution selling its assets is operating professionally before becoming confident on the future quality of the loans – whatever the statistics on past performance may be. Unless we had been able to convince the investors of the quality of the bank and its management, we would not have been able to securitise part of the Bulgarian loan portfolio. Hence, first ProCredit focuses on building the banks and their staff, enabling them to create and maintain a high-quality loan portfolio. Then, only as a second step, after having achieved a certain degree of "maturity", ProCredit would think about securitising assets.

Funding Costs

In principle, we do not see any specific advantages or disadvantages of structured finance solutions from a cost perspective. The securitisation in Bulgaria provided an attractive source of funding to the bank, especially as the bank has flexibility in terms of the volumes it could sell. Yet the overall costs entailed are in line with those for other sources of funding, i.e. securitisation was neither cheaper nor more expensive.

Outlook

The group will continue to use structured finance products to broaden its funding base, to fine-tune its asset-liability structure and to strengthen its equity base. Even during the financial crisis in 2008/2009, we managed to place complex Tier 1 and Tier 2 instruments with investors. However, these types of transactions will continue to play only a complementary role in the future within our overall deposit-focused funding and equity strategy. Within our range of financing options, structured finance solutions are simply one important component – no more, no less.

CHAPTER 11

Using the Toolbox – Solutions in Customizing Structured Finance

Richard Senior[*]

Robert is a plumber, and I am a carpenter. We have both worked in capital markets for many years. How can that be? Allow me to explain.

I was having a drink with Robert in a Canary Wharf bar some while back. He was at that time Head of Securitisation for a large bank, and I had left the world of big banks and set up Robin Hood Finance Ltd, a structured finance consultancy. The conversation turned to a common frustration in our business, the customer who asks about your specific experience in a very narrow area, such as (my caricature): *"how many deals based on loans to SMEs in South-Eastern Belgium and owned by left-handed Polish baseball players have you done …?"* Robert gave me his ready answer: *"I tell them that I'm a plumber. What does a plumber do? He has years of experience in dealing with water and pipes. Each case will be slightly different, and some may be very unusual, but the basic skills can be applied in every case. The plumber has to apply his knowledge and experience, and have at his disposal the right tools but very importantly, know how to use them"*.

By coincidence, I had developed a similar analogy. When asked about my experience, I would say that I am a carpenter, trained to work with all types of wood and have mastered the tools of my trade. I can recommend the structure that is best for the customer, the most suitable materials and the right price and where to obtain them and how to use them for construction.

A carpenter's tools include saws, chisels, and screwdrivers. A structured finance professional's tools include swaps, FX (foreign exchange), bonds and of course Credit Default Swaps (CDS). Warren Buffett is no fan of CDS, and is on record as describing them as *"financial weapons of mass destruction"*. However, any tool can be used for both, good or evil: The phrase *"stabbed with a screwdriver"* produces 822 hits on Google at the time of writing, but no-one to my knowledge has proposed a screwdriver ban. Or, as Thomas Huertas, a director at the Financial Services Authority (FSA) in London put it in a speech in April, 2008, *"Nuclear energy can create catastrophe or contribute to prosperity. Controls make the difference between Chernobyl and efficient energy. Whether nuclear energy has a future depends critically on whether controls can be effective"*. This applies equally to plumbers and carpenters.

In this chapter, I argue that there are many useful financial instruments, both traditional ones, and those which have been developed in the last few decades; that

---

[*] Director, Robin Hood Finance Ltd.

they are important tools in the toolbox and that they can be used and combined to produce the most efficient structure for each set of circumstances. I contrast the toolbox approach with the *"this worked in the US, so that must be the right way to do it here"* school of thought. Many of us suffered from this when building the European securitisation market, in the form of colleagues in New York who no doubt sincerely believed that what worked in the US must be exactly right for Europe, and indeed anywhere else.

Business Objective

The particular area we are concerned with here is improving funding and risk management to assist economic development in sub-investment grade countries. In other words, how can we use the tools at our disposal to bring together funders, risk takers and borrowers to get the most efficient deals for everyone?

The first stage is to identify clearly our objective. For example, assuming we are trying to get funding to corporate borrowers in a sub-investment grade country, there are a series of trade-offs. I have often asked customers whether they want the cheapest funding, or the maximum amount of funding. The answer is, of course, invariably "both"! This is an important part of identifying the boundaries of what constitutes a good deal for the customer.

A Solution in Search for a Problem?

We then have to search for the best structure. This is where we part company with those large investment banks that tend towards full securitisations for assets from sub-investment grade countries. A common scenario is, if a customer is marketed by a bank which sells bonds, they will strongly advise that a bond is the way to go. On the other hand, a bank that funds via a commercial paper conduit will be talking up its preferred distribution method. The bank acts primarily for itself, not for the customer.

What is a *"full securitisation"*? My simplified understanding is a deal put together by the securitisation group of one bank or another, bearing a striking resemblance to US or European mortgage, loan or some other well-established asset class. This involves

- the sale of assets to a Special Purpose Vehicle (SPV) in one of the usual locations such as Jersey, Caymans, Ireland, Luxembourg, the Netherlands …
- rating agency analysis
- swaps and other hedging provided by the arranger
- a (highly) rated bond issued in a major currency such as US Dollars (USD) or Euro (EUR).

In other words, this approach starts with what has been done before and tries to work out ways of replicating it in circumstances that are often very different. There is a Buddhist saying that a man who uses a raft to cross a river is wise; but a man who carries a raft on his back after he has crossed the river is a fool. Rather than start with the mindset that we have to do what has been done many times before in developed countries, we start with an open mind, identify each individual risk, and then find the most efficient tool to deal with that risk in order to put together the best deal.

Risks

Some of the risks the structurer has to deal with are (i) default, (ii) foreign exchange, (iii) interest rate and (iv) country ceiling. These are dealt with individually below, including tools we can use in each case:

Default

Default is a key risk in credit – the risk that the lender does not get his money back, because the debtor does not pay. The first stage in dealing with this is to identify exactly what the risk is. Is it, for example, the default risk of a single company, or group of companies in a single industry? Or are we dealing with a diversified pool of loans to individuals or firms? The easiest portfolios to analyse are those with very few or very many credits: a single debtor can be analysed using a traditional credit approach, and a diversified pool fits well with a securitisation-type approach. The traditional credit approach is what any bank should do before putting its shareholder's capital at risk: examining the business of the potential borrower, analysing the accounts, etc. A securitisation-type approach looks at a statistical mass of risks, such as mortgages or small loans, and uses past data to predict the probability of default in the future.

The quality of data is a challenge in the case of less developed countries. The first step in getting alternative finance in place is often to evaluate systems and procedures. This applies to all countries, but in general the lower the quality of systems and procedures, the greater the uncertainty to the risk-takers and therefore the worse the deal. In many cases, we have to get this right first.

There is also the Collateralized Debt Obligation (CDO)-type approach which can be used in corporate loans cases where there are a few dozen credits. In this case, each credit requires a rating (probability of default grade) which can be matched or mapped with a rating agency grade. This is described in detail as a case study in this chapter.

Risk Transfer Tools

Once we have identified the right approach to the risk, how can we transfer it? Various tools are at our disposal. Some of these that transfer risk also provide funding, whilst others transfer risk only in order to facilitate funding. A simple example of the former is a traditional loan: the lender puts up the money and has the risk of default. Bond insurance can serve as an example of the latter. This started in the municipal market in the US. Little-known, unrated municipalities could borrow from investors who require an AAA rating by enlisting an AAA-rated bond insurer. The bond insurer has a high, often AAA rating[1] and guarantees the bond: if the underlying issuer defaults, the insurer has to pay. It is a bit like a parent guaranteeing his student son or daughter's debt. Hence, the investor's risk is that both the underlying issuer *and* the bond insurer default. The economics work, because the AAA funding cost plus the insurance premium are less than the cost of borrowing in the municipality's own name.

We may have to consider using a number of tools to transfer risk, as in the trade finance case study below. This is not always easy when dealing with a typical investment bank and its bunker-mentality departments with, more often than we would like to see, their own departmental profit and loss statement uppermost in their minds. We might find that insurance adds value to the transaction, or that we can transfer risk with a credit default swap (CDS).

We then face the question which investors or risk-takers (including insurers, who might take risk but not provide funding) would be most interested in particular risks, and what their preferred format would be. There is no point in producing clever structures, if the end result is something which does not interest investors. For example, there might be plenty of USD investors, but fewer in the local currency; a large deal might go better with a rated bond, whilst a smaller one could be done as a private placement or bank syndication.

Foreign Exchange

One of the most difficult risks when dealing with sub-investment-grade countries is FX risk: the lender invariably does not have funding in the local currency, and wants an investment in USD, EUR or some other major currency. The borrower, on the other hand, often wants funding in his local currency. The usual approach in a securitisation is to put in place a currency swap. But the currency swap market between, say, Bangladeshi Taka and USD does not exist for practical purposes.

Deals have been done in the world of microfinance where the investment is made in a hard currency such as USD and the local originator's assets earn income in local currency with debt obligations in USD and exposing the local counterparties to the foreign exchange risks.

---

[1] There are some significant problems in this sector in the current financial market crisis.

So we go back to basics: where's the cash? It is usually found in the local country. This makes it possible to consider a structure where the money is lent locally, by a bank, fund or whatever other entity that has the cash to invest; and the risk is taken by an investor in a Western country. This could be in the form of a guarantee, or some form of parallel loan.

Another approach (again using Bangladesh as an example) is to ask the question who has USD income and Taka expenses? The answer would logically be Bangladeshi exporters. This offers an opportunity to examine the possibility of striking a deal with a domestic exporter who is long USD and short Taka. This is pretty much how deals were put together before the swap markets were established.

Interest Rate

In many structured financings there is a mismatch between the interest rates on the assets and that paid to investors. The traditional way of dealing with this is an interest rate swap: but what if there is no established market in the currency in which the deal is denominated? As with the FX risk, we can ask, who are natural receivers and payers of a fixed rate? For example, assume we have a book of leases which effectively pay a fixed rate, and we have to receive a floating rate to pay investors. So who would want to receive our fixed rate from the leases and pay us a floating rate? In the early days of the swap market, we would look for a local company that could borrow at an attractive fixed rate, but preferred to have a floating rate liability. A swap would be arranged along the following lines:

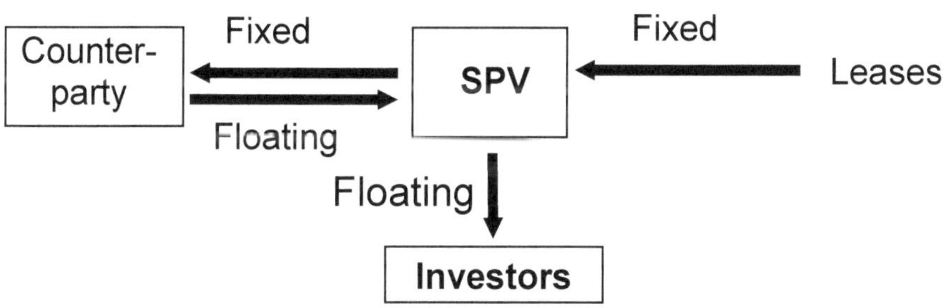

It is important to bear in mind that such approaches can be time-consuming to put in place, but also just asking a few investment banks to quote a price (or, even worse, taking whatever price is given by the derivatives department of a "partner" bank) is certainly no guarantee of getting the best deal. Both approaches should be explored.

Country Ceiling

The Country Ceiling is a problem when liabilities due from an entity in a country cannot be rated higher than the government of that country. This occurs when we are trying to produce AAA assets in a sub-investment grade country. The first question is: "*do we really need to produce AAA assets*"? If we do, as in the first case study below, we can examine alternative approaches such as certain kinds of insurance instruments. But if there are investors who will buy lower-rated or non-rated instruments, then the AAA objective is not essential. If the country in question is acceptable, to say Islamic investors for cultural or religious reasons, a Western rating is less important.

Another alternative is to use a form of the parallel loan structure previously mentioned, where cash is provided by a local bank, that in turn has protection from an international investor that has deposited USD in an escrow account. A variant would protect the local bank by a guarantee or CDS from an international investor. Thus, the cash is provided locally, but the risk is taken internationally. Each party takes the role for which it is best suited.

Case Studies

Some of these points can be illustrated by the approach taken in the following cases.

Case 1: Trade Finance Receivables

How can various tools be combined in a non-traditional way to get a deal done to the satisfaction of all parties?

A firm with a book of receivables from sub-investment grade countries sought help to raise alternative funding through securitisation. At first sight, this looks like a tall order:

- There were fewer than 20 receivables, hardly a statistical pool, but on the other hand a lot to be analysed individually.
- All the receivables were 3–5 years, due from sub-investment grade countries which creates a country ceiling problem. As noted above, this means in general that obligations from any debtor in a country cannot have a better rating than the government of that country (you don't expect to get AAA risk from a BB country).
- The amounts due were in three major currencies, payable on irregular dates throughout the life of the assets.
- The portfolio was around USD 50 million, which is not really big enough for a bond deal.

This was the starting point:

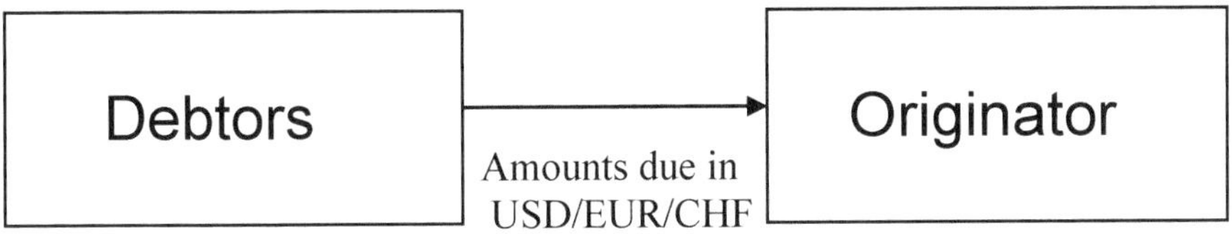

This portfolio was therefore quite unsuitable for a "full securitisation". So, we reached for our toolbox, and tried to identify the best way of dealing with each risk in order to put together a viable deal.

Since we could not do a statistical analysis, and because it was impractical to do detailed credit work involving due diligence trips to several countries on each asset, we looked at the possibility of insurance. Bond insurers (often called monolines) do not take the sort of risk we were dealing with; they insure or "wrap" risks which are already of a rated standard. What other insurers could we approach? The solution was credit and political risk (CPR) insurers, whose business it is to cover risks from just the type of sub-investment grade countries we were dealing with. We negotiated a policy whereby the insurer (A rated) would cover all of the assets, with a 10% first-loss piece retained by the originator. The fee for this was quite high but so was the yield on the assets, and the economics worked. This was the position after having negotiated the CPR insurance:

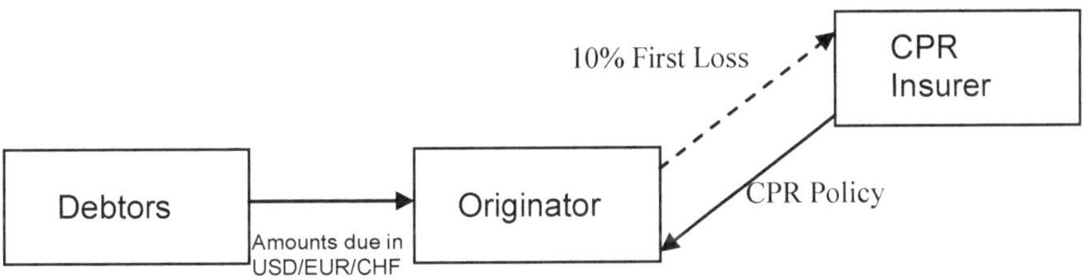

So far so good, but we still did not have an instrument we could sell to an investor. For one thing, there was a problem with the type of insurance. Capital market investors want to see an unequivocal obligation to pay on the due date. Traditional insurers, as everyone who has claimed on a car or home insurance policy will attest, require a claim to be completed, and may refuse to pay in part or in full if they consider that some term of the policy has not been complied with. This is the difference between *"pay first, ask questions later"*, and *"ask questions first, pay later"*. Capital markets investors set little value on traditional insurance for this reason.

We needed a party with a high rating who would agree to pay when due with none of the *"wriggle room"* which insurers have. One possibility was banks, but the banks' pricing was prohibitive. We looked at insurance more deeply, since insurers understand insurers, and identified a reinsurance company prepared to guarantee the risk at an acceptable price.

The next step was to isolate the assets from the originator, making them *"bankruptcy remote"* from the estate of the originator. There seemed to be no reason not to use the traditional SPV structure, and Ireland was the chosen location due to its favourable tax regime for both SPV taxation and cross-border tax. Hence we had reached the following position:

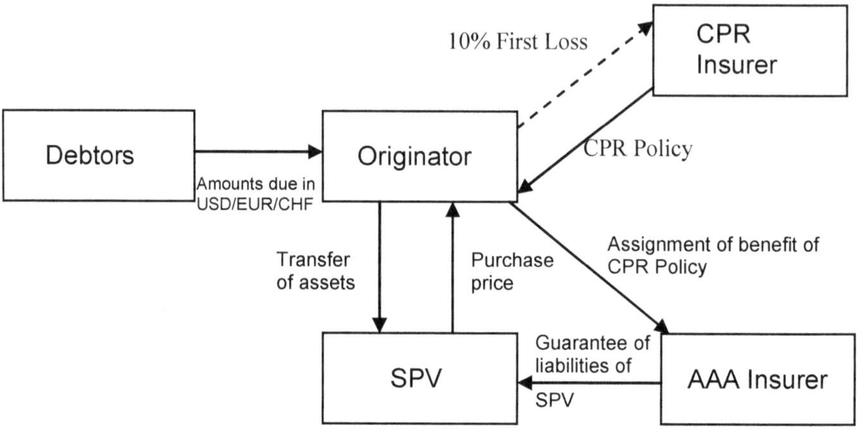

Note that the AAA insurer guarantees the liabilities of the SPV, not just the assets. This is important, since there are other parties to the transaction (e.g. the swap bank introduced below) who need to know who their counterparty is and the credit quality provided.

In two steps, we have come from sub-investment grade debt in developing countries to AAA risk, and in a rather unusual way. As noted above, conventional securitisation would simply not have worked, so we used different tools creatively. But there are a few more risks to be dealt with before the transaction can be sold to investors. The cash flows are in three currencies and payable on odd dates. Investors like to invest in a single currency and have regular cash flows. Hence, we designed a swap under which the cash flows from the assets (or from the AAA insurer if the assets failed!) are paid into a swap, and regular quarterly payments representing principal and interest to investors are paid back to the SPV.

One further party was required: the insurer might be good for the money, but being an insurer and not a bank, would it have the money available at two days' notice? It was necessary to add a liquidity line from a bank, which would make payments as required, then re-claim from the AAA insurer.

Once we achieved an AAA risk and dealt with the cash flows, we finally had an amortising USD bond with an AAA (private) rating which could be sold to investors. The final form of the transaction was as follows:

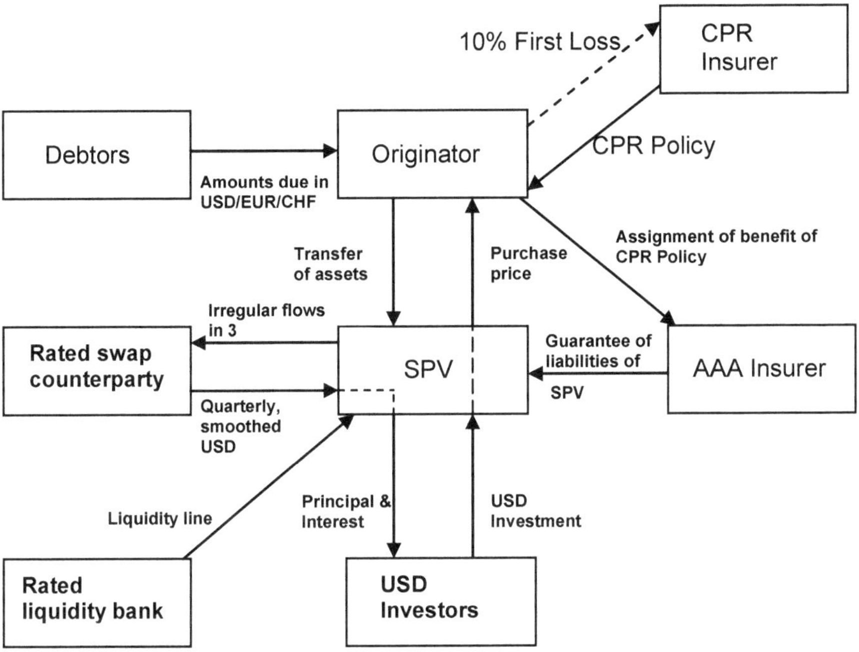

A somewhat unorthodox transaction, but by dealing with each risk individually and finding the best way to manage it, a good result was achieved. In the same way, this transaction should not be considered as a blueprint for any other deal.

The approach taken, not the final structure, is important. That's how the carpenter and the plumber work.

Case 2: B+ Rated Country Car Leases

A leasing company in a B+ rated country locally leases cars to companies. The leasing company was partly funded by local banks, and partly by the (foreign) parent. In this case, the task was to see whether more than USD 100 million of lease receivables from a B+ country could be financed via securitisation in order to get alternative term funding, and reduce dependency on the parent.

The leasing company had enlisted a local bank a year earlier to assess the possibility of a securitisation. This bank concentrated on the monthly amounts due from the lessees, and tried to analyse these in the same way as a mortgage pool. This analysis was inadequate for several reasons:

Concentrations. A mortgage pool has thousands of similar assets, none of which forms more than a fraction of a percentage of the total. This pool had significant concentrations, single names as a proportion of the total pool. The top 25 customers contributed over half of the pool. This does not constitute a statistical pool:

several individual assets are that large as a proportion of the whole that they must be analysed individually.

A CDO analysis is usually the best way to analyse a book of corporate obligors when there are relatively few of them. CDO analysis differs from other approaches, because it does not consider past pool performance. It starts with a risk grade for each debtor, such as BBB-, B+ or whatever is appropriate to the customer as described in more detail below. The model then adds in the other key factor, which is correlation or co-variance. This is the rating agency's estimate of how likely company B is to default if company A has defaulted. Common sense tells us that, if one US motor manufacturer goes bust, then another has a strong probability of suffering the same fate, so the correlation is high. On the other hand, an Italian life insurance company would normally have a low correlation with a US motor manufacturer.

Residual Values. The analysis ignored a key factor in car leasing, which is that cars do not decline to a zero value, but are sold after 2 or 3 years when the lease has expired. This is a large part of the financing requirement: in effect, financing future cash flows from sales into the used car market. Securitisations have been devised from each of the types of payments due from lessees: the monthly cash flows and Residual values (RV). A German example is League 2005-1 Ltd. in which separate series of notes funded the monthly lease payments and the residual values.

Structure. The bank spent quite some time analysing whether a conduit or a master trust would be the more appropriate funding source. My answer was a) neither, and b) get the assets in securitisable form before concerning ourselves with such points.

The first hurdle in any transaction, especially in a non-investment grade country where securitisation is not common, is to make the assets acceptable to investors or, their proxies, rating agencies.

During a visit to the leasing company's head office, the answer to the question *"what credit procedures do you use?"* was, somewhat surprisingly, *"none"*. This was unexpected. I asked for further background. The approach was quite simple: if a customer asked about leasing, say, 50 cars for 3 years, the leasing company would approach several local banks and ask the banks whether and at what price they would factor the monthly payments. If the bank said yes, the deal was done. If the bank said no, the deal was not done.

Such a procedure was not, unfortunately, of any use in convincing an investor that this was a reasonable risk. So being a couple of steps back, we had to think about how to put acceptable credit procedures in place that would be acceptable to third parties. There were three possibilities:

- external rating of each customer by a rating agency (unlikely),
- internal rating (not done at present, but the leasing company had considered moving in this direction),

- proxy rating (Dun & Bradstreet, etc., or a rating agency scoring model such as S&P's Credit Risk Tracker).

The objective was to have a measure of probability of default which was sufficiently objective to be acceptable to a rating agency or external investor.

After much discussion, the company decided to install a system based on one used by a local bank. The residual values, a significant proportion of the funding requirement, had also used a "seat of the pants" approach. As with the corporate risk, this approach would not convince raters and investors: proper, objective systems and procedures had to be put in place. This is Moody's description of what information it obtained in one rated residual value deal:

> *"Moody's has been provided with static historical residual value performance data on the historical pool for the period starting from 1996. In addition, Moody's also received contract-by-contract data (excluding defaulted leases) on the historical residual value performance (sample size over 13,600), which includes the following information:*
>
> - *the leased vehicles' value and calculated residual value at the beginning of the lease;*
> - *sale proceeds, proceeds arising from excessive mileage and damage costs, payments and proceeds arising from extension of the lease agreement;*
> - *date of lease origination;*
> - *manufacturer and model of the leased vehicle.*

A consultant specialised in the auto leasing industry was brought in, and helped in designing and implementing market-standard procedures for the firm as a whole, including how RVs are set and managed.

How do we fund such a portfolio, assuming we have good systems and information? This case is still in process, but some of the main options were based on the fact that traditional ABS might be difficult in a B+ country. How is it possible to get an AAA rating, not only for the monthly flows and residual values, but also for swaps, FX and indeed all other risks? The tool we used in the earlier case was CPR insurance plus an AAA wrap, but that proved to be expensive in this case.

Thinking outside traditional securitisation, we changed the question from how do we get an AAA rating to how do we find acceptable funding for the leasing company? One approach was local funding, with the risk taken by investors in higher-rated countries:

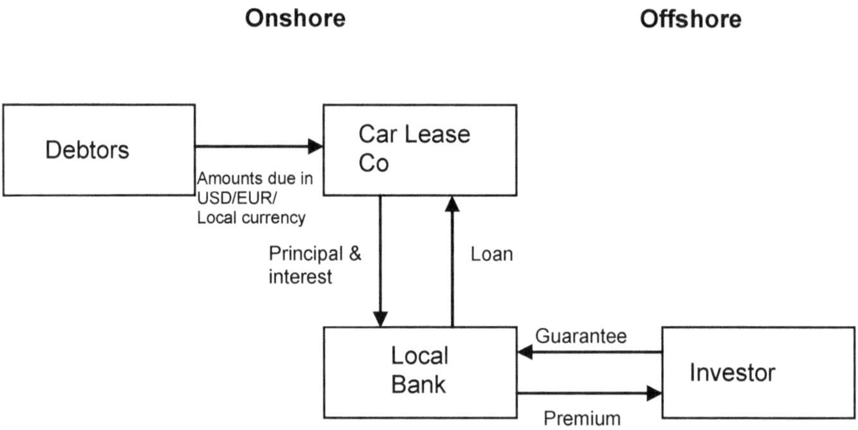

The advantage here was that the funding could be done locally, whilst the actual risk could be taken by a highly-rated investor. Thus, the local bank funds the local leasing company, but the ultimate risk-taker is offshore, giving the bank a highly-rated risk.

This is an attractive approach in principle, but it proved difficult to identify an appropriate local bank. This might have been due to the philosophy common to protectionist-minded bankers throughout the world *"... but I'd be cannibalising my own business"*.

The preferred approach was Islamic financing. Shari'ah law forbids the making and taking of payments of interest, but cars and payment for their use represent an underlying *"real"* transaction which can be made acceptable to Islamic investors. These investors are also not as ratings-driven as Western investors, so it is possible to be more creative in putting structures together. Finally, there is a significant pool of funds looking for a Shari'ah-compliant home financing estimated to exceed USD 700 billion[2]. Islamic financing is generally seen as a significant growth area, and, as Standard and Poor's put it in the title of a paper: *"Islamic Finance Is Securitization's New Frontier"*.[3]

Conclusion

Trying to replicate developed countries' approaches to structuring AAA ABS bonds for risks in developing countries may be possible, but it is by no means the only possible approach. The traditional ABS approach should not be seen as the

---

[2] Moody's, in a 2008 paper entitled "2007 Review and 2008 Outlook: Islamic Finance: Sukuk Take Centre Stage, Other Shariah-Compliant Products Gain Popularity as Demand Increases".

[3] See contributions of Andreas Jobst and Paul Ali, also in this volume.

target. A better approach is to examine the various risks and determine which parties can most efficiently assume them, and then use the tools in our toolbox to build the best structure. A note of caution: an unskilled worker, even with the best tools available, easily ends up drilling through the water pipe, or short-circuiting the electrical system. Get professional plumbers and carpenters in.

CHAPTER 12

Microcredit as an Asset Class: Structured Microfinance

Literature Review and Perspectives

Gregor Dorfleitner, Michaela Leidl, and Christopher Priberny[*]

Abstract

Microfinance is perceived as evolving from philanthropy to an investment opportunity, with a potential growth of funds into microfinance institutions (MFIs). Microfinance investors are either commercially or socially motivated. Commercial investors comprise investment funds, individual investors (including high net-worth individuals), and financial institutions. Socially motivated investors expect that their investments will provide social benefits to specified target groups or activities, while achieving sustainable financial returns. These investors include donor organizations, development finance and international finance institutions, and private investors.

Investors may be attracted by the lack of correlation of microfinance portfolios and other asset classes as well as the growing importance of regulated MFIs. Microfinance investment funds (MFIFs) and securitization of microfinance portfolios have become additional vehicles for expanding investment in microfinance. MFIs' attractiveness in capital markets is often undermined by unreliable data of some MFIs, although even unsecured MFI asset portfolios are usually of high quality. However, the global financial crisis of 2008/2009 has pointed to vulnerabilities of microfinance in some countries. A survey addressed to microfinance experts operating worldwide appears to support a positive outlook for structured microfinance despite the ongoing crisis.

Introduction

The perception of microfinance (MF) has changed from philanthropy to an investment opportunity. A few years ago, MF was largely seen as a means to reduce poverty and boost the economies of developing countries. Today, MF offers an

[*] Department of Finance, University of Regensburg.

attractive investment opportunity for diverse types of investors, although this change is subject to controversial debate. For example, Nobel Peace Prize Winner Muhammad Yunus[1] refers to investors in lucrative microfinance instruments as the new moneylenders.

Anyway, there appears to remain an immense gap between the demand and supply of MF. Daley-Harris[2] refers to an estimated demand of USD 300 billion, while MFIs reporting to MIX Market were only able to supply a gross loan portfolio of approximately USD 44 billion in 2008.[3] As a result, private investments will be critical for meeting the enormous and fast-growing demand for MF.

Whether MF is already an asset class is currently under debate. Greer[4] defines an asset class as a *"[...] set of assets that bear some fundamental economic similarities to each other, and that have characteristics that make them distinct from other assets that are not part of that class."* Whereas Reddy and Rhyne[5] as well as Swanson[6] do not yet regard MF as a separate asset class, Ananth[7] considers MF to be exactly that.

This chapter presents different MF investment instruments for various types of investors. First, we provide a stylized classification of MF investors. Second, we define and discuss the MF investment instruments currently available. Third, we examine the suitability of these instruments for different types of investors and place special emphasis on structured microfinance. Furthermore, we discuss several problems to be solved in structured microfinance and offer perspectives for solutions in theory and practice. Finally, we present the results of a survey on structured MF instruments.

---

1 See Yunus, Muhammad (2007): Remarks by Muhammad Yunus. In: Microcredit Summit E-News Bulletin 5(1), http://www.microcreditsummit.org/enews/index.html.

2 See Daley-Harris, Sam (2009): State of the microcredit summit campaign report 2009, p. 10. Microcredit Summit Campaign, Washington D.C.

3 See Gonzalez, Adrian (2009): Microfinance at a glance – 2008, MicroFinance Information eXchance, Washington D.C.

4 See Greer, Robert J. (1997): What is an asset class anyway? in: Journal of Portfolio Management 23(2), p. 86.

5 See Reddy, Rekha; Rhyne, Elisabeth (2006): Who will buy our paper: Microfinance cracking the capital markets? The realities of linking microfinance to local and international markets, pp. 12–13. InSight No. 18, Acción.

6 See Swanson, Brad (2007): The role of international capital markets in microfinance, Working Paper, Research Symposium "Credit Markets for the Poor", p. 13. Columbia Business School, New York.

7 See Ananth, Bindu (2005): Financing microfinance – the ICICI Bank partnership model. In: Small Enterprise Development 16(1), p. 62.

Types of MF Investors and Their Requirements

There are two main categories of MF investors: the commercial and the socially motivated. Although we implement a rather clear distinction between socially motivated and commercial investors in this chapter, this does not mean that there are no overlaps in reality. Needless to say, commercial investors can at the same time follow social motives.

Figure 1 provides an overview of the different types. We take the view of de Sousa-Shields[8] who classifies commercial investors into defined liability and institutional funds, individual investors, and financial institution lenders.[9]

So-called defined liability and institutional funds are either public or private pension funds, insurance funds, trusts, mutual funds, or other funds managed by private institutions. Two types of individual investors can be distinguished: high

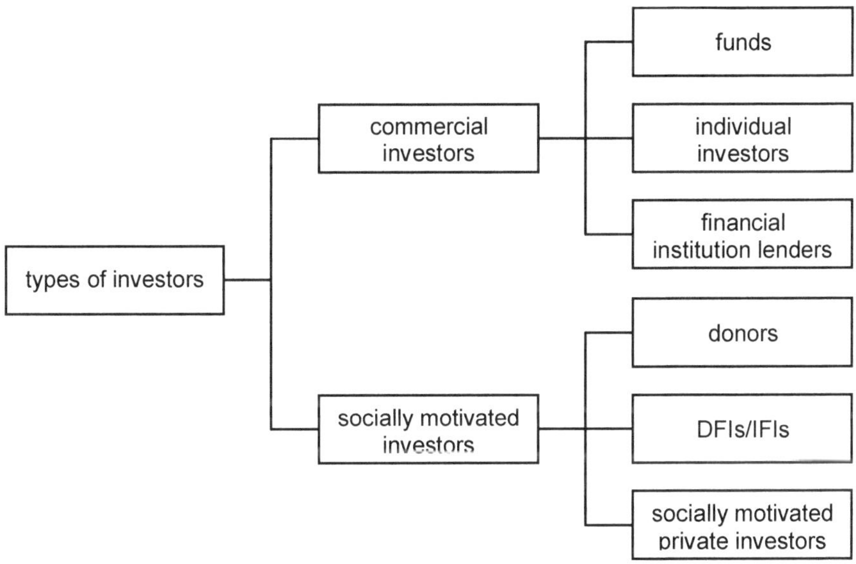

Fig. 1. Types of MF investors

8 See de Sousa-Shields, Marc (2006): Commercial investment in microfinance: A class by itself? In: Matthäus-Maier, I./von Pischke, J.D. (Eds.): Microfinance investment funds: Leveraging private capital for economic growth and poverty reduction. Berlin (a.o.): Springer, 81–93.

9 In addition to these types of investors, de Sousa-Shields (2006) considers local depositors as commercial investors. According to Ledgerwood and White (2006, p. 164), MFIs mobilize savings from local clients by transforming from NGOs into regulated financial institutions. Although the importance of deposits as funding source for MFIs is rising and voluntary deposits of MFIs accounted for more than USD 16 billion in 2008 (Gonzalez, 2009), we do not regard depositors as commercial investors.

net-worth individuals (HNWIs) and investors with modest portfolios. Financial-institution lenders are banks and non-bank financial institutions.

Having discussed commercial investors, we now observe socially motivated investors. This group consists of donors, development finance institutions (DFIs) and international finance institutions (IFIs), as well as socially motivated private investors.

Donors may be classified as official (bilateral and multilateral agencies) and private donors (foundations, non-governmental organizations (NGOs), etc.). DFIs include development agencies and development banks. The group of socially motivated private investors comprises, for example, private foundations.

Different types of investors have different expectations regarding the return on an investment opportunity depending on their time horizon and the degree of risk they are willing to tolerate.[10]

The behavior of commercial investors is strongly affected by quantitative asset-allocation strategies. The objective of these strategies is not so much to reduce the risk of a certain asset, but rather the risk management of the whole portfolio [11]. According to empirical studies of individual investor behavior, risk tolerance is negatively correlated with the investor's age.[12] The investment style of HNWIs highly depends on their personal interests. Financial institution lenders attach great importance to collateral, but MFIs cannot provide collateral in most cases. Another important factor for financial institution lenders is the transparency of an MFI as reflected by supervision and the rating of MFIs by major rating agencies.

In contrast to commercial investors, social investors demand a social return in addition to the financial return.[13] For donors, development objectives such as promoting financial-sector development and extending the frontiers of development finance are of primary importance. The requirements of DFIs and IFIs combine development objectives and a financial return. Among the objectives of socially motivated private investors, an appropriate financial return ranks next to a social return.

Next, we examine the preferences of different types of investors, particularly regarding the risk of an investment opportunity. Most MF investors seek diversification from other asset classes. They are aware of risk and return, requiring an adequate return for a certain risk. Commercial microfinance investors are gener-

---

[10] See Ledgerwood, Joanna; White, Victoria (2006): Transforming microfinance institutions: Providing full financial services to the poor, p. 168, Washington D.C.: World Bank.

[11] See de Sousa-Shields, Marc (2006): Commercial investment in microfinance: A class by itself? In: Matthäus-Maier, I./von Pischke, J.D. (Eds.): Microfinance investment funds: Leveraging private capital for economic growth and poverty reduction. Berlin (a.o.): Springer, pp. 81–85.

[12] See Hallahan, Terrence; Faff, Robert; McKenzie, Michael (2003): An exploratory investigation of the relation between risk tolerance scores and demographic characteristics. In: Journal of Multinational Financial Management 13(4–5), pp. 494–495.

[13] See op. cit de Sousa-Shields, Marc (2006) pp. 90–91.

ally highly risk-sensitive.[14] The risk tolerance of individual investors depends on their age and individual preferences. The risk tolerance of mutual funds – a subgroup of defined liability and institutional funds – is variable, since each fund pursues its own investment policy.[15]

Financial institution lenders have a rather variable risk tolerance that attempts to match the risk of their assets to the risk of their liabilities.[16] The risk related to the group of socially motivated investors also depends on the specific type of socially motivated investor. Donors can be seen as risk-takers, since they feature lower risk sensitivity to losses. The risk-sensitivity of DFIs and IFIs is somewhat higher. Due to regulatory limitations, some DFIs are more risk adverse in contrast to IFIs. Socially motivated private investors are highly risk averse, as are the group of commercial investors.

MF Investment Instruments and Their Suitability for Investors

Overview

MFIs have access to several funding sources for their MF portfolios. They can borrow funds and issue bonds or equity, and thus create various ways of investing in MF. De Sousa-Shields[17] differentiates between direct and indirect investments. In this section, we describe alternatives of direct investments in equity and debt of MFIs, and indirect investment through MFIFs. Special emphasis is placed on structured microfinance.

Equity Financing

According to Ledgerwood and White,[18] MFIs have access to further capital sources by transforming from NGOs into regulated financial institutions, since transformation generally implies the creation of a shareholding company. After transformation, the equity base of an MFI no longer consists mainly of grants. Instead it includes a combination of share capital and retained earnings.

The search for new shareholders becomes increasingly important when MFIs transform into regulated entities, because they have to fulfill banking supervisory requirements. In this regard, the presence of strategic investors other than the original NGO is essential. However, in most cases the NGO retains a major part of

[14] See Byström, Hans (2008): The microfinance collateralized debt obligation: A modern Robin Hood. In: World Development 36(11), p. 2112.

[15] See Bodie, Zvi; Kane, Alex; Marcus, Alan J. (2005): Investments, New York: McGraw-Hill, pp. 112 and 941.

[16] See op.cit. Bodie, Zvi; Kane, Alex; Marcus, Alan J. (2005), pp 941 and 943.

[17] See op. cit Sousa-Shields, Marc (2006), p. 82.

[18] See op. cit. Ledgerwood, Joanna; White, Victoria (2006) p. 184.

the shares of its related MFI. Further shareholders are, for example, semi-commercial specialized funds, multi- or bilateral donors, and international NGOs. The investors' demand for MFI equity is limited due to low exit opportunities.[19]

Share issuance generally occurs through public offerings or private placements. Initial public offerings (IPOs) have appeared in the microfinance industry only recently. The first public issues were the MFI Bank Rakyat Indonesia in 2003 and the IPO of the Equity Bank, Kenya in 2006.[20] Further examples are IPOs of Mibanco in Peru and BancoSol in Bolivia[21] as well as of Network Microfinance Bank in Pakistan. Rhyne and Guimon describe in detail the IPO of Compartamos, a Mexican MFI with over 1,500,000 clients.[22] Although IPOs are relatively new and uncommon in the microfinance industry, they have been quite successful. However, the Compartamos IPO has triggered a debate about high profit taking of investors taking advantage of excessive lending margins vis-à-vis their micro enterprise borrowers.[23]

Debt Financing

There are several commercial investment opportunities in MFI debt, namely term loans and lines of credit, subordinated and convertible debt as well as bonds.[24]

Term loans and lines of credit are common types of investments. Investors including local foundations, international funds specializing in microfinance, local governments, international financial institutions, and commercial banks provide these funding sources. Subordinated debt is more risky than term loans and credit lines, which means that investors will require higher interest rates. Subordinated debt is often convertible into equity.[25]

MFI bonds often carry a higher risk than secured loans, but are less risky than investments in MFI equity. Bonds are offered to investors through private placements or through public offerings. The market for private placements is limited because of risk and an illiquid secondary market. Consequently, the number of potential buyers is narrow, making the costs of private placements higher. Investors in private placements are, for example, institutional investors such as banks, mutual funds, insurance companies, pension funds, and foundations. There are fewer

---

[19] See Jansson, Tor (2003): Financing microfinance: Exploring the funding side of microfinance institutions, Inter-American Development Bank, Sustainable Development Department Technical Paper Series, Washington D.C, pp. 9–13.

[20] See Rhyne, Elisabeth; Guimon, Andres (2007): The Banco Compartamos initial public offering, InSight No. 23, Acción, p. 11.

[21] See op. cit. Ledgerwood, Joanna; White, Victoria (2006) p. 186.

[22] See Compartamos (2010): Social, economic and human value: Strengths to keep on growing – annual report 2009, Banco Compartamos S.A., Mexico, p. 2.

[23] See CGAP Premium.

[24] See op. cit. Ledgerwood, Joanna; White, Victoria (2006), pp. 176–184.

[25] See op. cit. Ledgerwood, Joanna;White, Victoria, pp. 178–181.

potential investors in private placements than there are in public offerings. The first private placements of bonds were issued in 1996 and 1997 by BancoSol. In 2002 and 2003, Compartamos issued three privately placed bonds.

MFI debt through public bond offerings is most extensively used by investors. Compartamos made a public bond offering in 2004.[26] Lopez[27] describes in detail the bond offerings of Mibanco and Compartamos.

Microfinance Investment Funds

According to Goodman,[28] there are three basic forms of MFIFs: microfinance development funds, quasi-commercial MFIFs, and commercial MFIFs. Microfinance development funds' predominant purpose is the development and growth of MFIs. Investors in these types of funds are basically donors, development agencies, private investors and corporations. Although the investors aim to maintain the inflation-adjusted value of their investment, they regard the social return as being more important.

Quasi-commercial MFIFs in contrast seek financial returns targeting private donors and development agencies.

A third type of MFIF is purely commercially oriented. These primarily target commercial investors, both private and institutional. Commercial MFIFs tend to have clearer objectives than other funds, because commercial investors require more detailed better quality information and greater transparency.[29] Commercial MFIFs aim to offer a financial return while maintaining development objectives. Table 1 below provides an overview of the different types of investors that generally invest in MFIFs.

Goodman[30] explains the advantages of MFIFs. Allocation to a wider group of MFIs improves risk diversification. Moreover, MFIFs can target investors' motives. For example, if an MFIF wants to target commercial investors, it ought to invest in sustainable MFIs in order to generate a sufficient financial return and meet their requirements. If socially-motivated investors should be targeted, also younger MFIs can be funded. MFIFs may encourage competition among MFIs, providing incentives for financial discipline that also has a positive impact on MFIs' returns. Moreover, MFIFs may offer more flexible decision-making processes than, for example, donor agencies.

---

26 See op. cit. Ledgerwood, Joanna;White, Victoria p. 182–183.

27 See Lopez, Cecar (2005): Microfinance approaches the bond market – the cases of Mibanco and Compartamos. In: Small Enterprise Development 16(1), p. 57.

28 See Goodman, Patrick (2006): Microfinance investment funds: Objectives, players, potential. In: Matthäus-Maier, I./von Pischke, J.D. (Eds.): Microfinance investment funds: Leveraging private capital for economic growth and poverty reduction. Berlin (a.o.): Springer, pp. 26–28.

29 See op. cit. Goodman, Patrick, pp. 26–27.

30 See op. cit. Goodman, Patrick, pp. 34–35.

Microfinance Securitization

Maurer[31] defines and provides a general introduction and overview to structured microfinance. Taxonomies vary: Byström[32] cites direct and indirect securitization, while Jobst[33] identifies three basic types of structured microfinance: MFIFs, direct securitization or local issuance, and indirect securitization or external issuance. Glaubitt et al.[34] also see no limitation of structured finance to securitization. The elements of structured finance can as well be applied to MFIFs. Hence, MFIFs offer a combination of flexible management by private fund managers and the techniques of structured finance, e.g. tranching. Glaubitt et al. show the structure of such MFIFs, using the European Fund for Southeast Europe as an example.

Indirect securitization transactions are more frequent than direct transactions. The most frequent forms of structured microfinance indirect securitizations are collateralized debt obligations (CDOs). Tranching can create different risk-return profiles within the possibilities of the asset pool and instruments and hence attracts varied types of investors as illustrated in Table 1 below.[35]

Tranching also addresses the problem of asymmetrical information. Generally, the originator of a securitization has an information advantage over the investor regarding the quality of the loans in the underlying asset pool. This problem can be solved by offering the safe senior tranches to the less informed investors with a lower risk-tolerance level, with the originator retaining the risky equity tranche.[36] Another benefit is that a particular transaction can be tailored to the requirements of a specific type of investor. There are also benefits from the diversification of the underlying asset pool with respect to the activities of the micro borrowers and geographic locations of the MFIs.[37] Moreover, MFs have very homogenous maturities and credit amounts, making them perfectly appropriate for securitization. For an overview of the advantages of structured microfinance we recommend Dorfleitner and Priberny.[38]

---

[31] See op. cit. Maurer, Klaus (2011).

[32] See op. cit. Byström, Hans (2008), p. 27.

[33] See Jobst, Andreas A. (2011): Structured Finance for Development – Outlook for New Applications, in this volume.

[34] See Glaubitt, Klaus; Hagen, Hanns Martin; Feist, Johannes; Beck, Monika (2008): Reducing barriers to microfinance investments: The role of structured finance. In: Matthäus-Maier, I./von Pischke, J.D. (Eds.): New partnerships for innovation in microfinance, Berlin (a.o.): Springer, pp. 360.

[35] See op. cit. Byström, Hans (2008), p. 2112.

[36] See op. cit. Byström, Hans (2008), p. 2115.

[37] See Hüttenrauch, Harald; Schneider, Claudia (2008): Securitisation: A funding alternative for microfinance institutions. In: Matthäus-Maier, I./von Pischke, J.D. (Eds.): New partnerships for innovation in microfinance. Berlin (a.o.): Springer, 299–347.

[38] See Dorfleitner, Gregor; Priberny, Christopher (2010): A quantitative model for structured microfinance, Working Paper, University of Regensburg.

Risk-Return Properties

Koivulehto[39] examines the profitability of MF, comparing the credit spreads on the MF portfolios of 24 MFIs in 14 countries with the spreads of exchange-traded USD-corporate bonds having equal levels of risk between 1997 and 2005. The results of the quantitative analysis show that the return of the 24 MFIs was 7.41 percentage points lower than demanded by USD-investors at a 95% significance level with a standard deviation of 30.34 percentage points. She concludes that MFI-specific factors are more important than the operating environment for the profitability of an MFI. The write-off ratio is used as a proxy to determine the average probability of default. The write-off ratio averages 1.72% with a standard deviation of 2.83% and depends heavily on the regional location of the MFI. The qualitative analysis reveals that the MFIs with the best performance have several years of experience, commercially oriented sources of capital, a defined target market, and transformed from NGOs into regulated organizations.

Krauss and Walter[40] empirically investigate the correlation of microfinance with global and local market movements. They compare 283 MFIs based in 65 emerging-market countries to 105 emerging-market commercial banks in 22 countries which are used as a benchmark. They examine key variables such as the net operating income and changes in five further variables. Return on equity and profit margin served as profitability indicators. Changes in total assets and changes in gross loan portfolio were used as indicators for changes in the value of bank assets. Loan portfolio at risk, i.e. over 30 days past-due served as an indicator of asset quality. They examine the correlation of these variables with global capital markets (i.e. the S&P 500 Index, the MSCI World Equities Index, and the MSCI Emerging Markets Index) and the domestic economy both for MFIs and commercial banks. The results confirm that MFIs display a low correlation to other asset classes. MFIs, for example, do not show a significant correlation with the S&P 500 index regarding either of the observed variables. According to Krauss and Walter, microfinance investments are useful for portfolio diversification.

These investigations deal with the asset side of MFIs' balance sheets. How risk and return of the assets are transferred to the liability side is a question of the capital structure and therefore the financing of the MFIs. In this view, every investment instrument (even bonds, loans, shares, etc.) is a means of structuring the asset side (i.e. the microcredit portfolio). Structured MF may be most suited to transforming the risk-return profile in any manner desired, while due to diversification, the risk-return relation should generally become more beneficial. Still, one can hope that in structuring, the low correlation relationship remains valid. However,

---

39 See Koivulehto, Hanna K. (2007): Should we invest in microcredit? A financial analysis of microcredit from a USD-investor's perspective, September 2007, Vienna University of Economics and Business Administration, Working Paper.

40 See Krauss, Nicolas; Walter, Ingo (2009): Can microfinance reduce portfolio volatility?, Economic Development and Cultural Change 58(1) (1 October 2009).

if a Microfinance CDO (MiCDO) embraces MFIs or MFs from different countries, the foreign exchange (FX) influence is an additional source of risk.[41]

Furthermore, the risk-return profiles of MFI stocks as well as their correlation with other asset classes have not yet been subject to empirical studies. This issue should be investigated when a sufficient number of MFIs are listed on stock exchanges.

Suitability for Types of Investors

Having introduced the different types of investors and the various MF investment opportunities, we now discuss the suitability of various instruments for different types of investors.

Equity donations are insufficient to close the gap between supply and demand of microcredit, because investments are undertaken only if investors seek solely a social return.

In contrast, equity shares have the potential to offer their investors a financial return. While many different types of investors are shareholders of MFIs, only a limited number of MFIs are able to offer their shares to investors. The equity of MFIs organized as NGOs primarily consists of equity-donations and retained earnings, if an MFI is financially sustainable. Few MFIs have been transformed into regulated financial institutions and only a negligible fraction has accomplished an IPO. However, some have sold relatively illiquid shares. According to Ledgerwood and White[42], the condition for the transformation of most MFIs is the issuance of shares. Hence, it is easier for transformed MFIs to sell their equity. Because transformation is still rare, donated equity is yet more common. Investments in MFI equity will be facilitated, if the number of IPOs accomplished by MFIs increases. Bonds are an interesting investment possibility, especially for commercial investors. However, financial markets in developing countries are mostly too undeveloped for such products. MFIFs and structured MF have the ability to attract most types of investors, because they offer many advantages. MFIFs provide funding sources for many different MFIs in various countries, which create a high level of diversification. With structured MF, various risk-return profiles can be created. Hence, a broad variety of investors is able to invest in structured finance independently of their particular risk tolerance. Furthermore, MiCDOs have a special advantage: the problems of information asymmetries can be reduced by the originator's retaining the equity tranche.

Table 1 sums up the relationships by connecting the types of investors with the instruments to which they are most attracted. Here, MFIFs are simultaneously an investment instrument and an investor type, because of their intermediation function. From the MFIs' view, they undoubtedly are investors, from other investors' point of view they are potential investment instruments. We find that structured

---

41 See op. cit. Byström, Hans (2008).

42 See op. cit. Ledgerwood, Joanna;White, Victoria (2006), p. 184.

Table 1. Investments of different types of investors

	Equity donations	Equity shares	Loans	Bonds	MFIFs	Structured MF
Funds		×	○	×	×	×
Individual investors		×		×	×	×
Financial institution lenders		×	×	×	○	×
Donors	×		×		×	×
DFIs/IFIs		×	×		×	×
Socially motivated private investors		○		○	×	×
MFIFs		×	×	○	○	×

Combinations labeled with '×' are based on actual MF investments described in various sources. Combinations marked with '○' are also possible.

microfinance products fit the objectives of most types of investors. Therefore, they are recommended as 'ideal' investment products.

Future Perspectives

In practice, several theoretical and practical problems need to be addressed to increase the dissemination of structured MF products. We conclude with an outline of these problems:[43]

- The microfinance sector currently produces only a small amount of reliable data. To investigate aspects of MF as an asset class and, in particular, properties of different MF investment instruments such as structured instruments, it is essential to build a database covering as many MFIs for as many years as possible. Such a database should contain returns, empirical default rates, risk capital, spreads of MFIs and real transaction prices of investments into MF-related instruments. The data published by MIX Market can be a starting point. However, it covers only MFIs and MFIFs to a limited extent and with variable data quality. The existence of such a database surely would boost academic research on MF as an asset class.

[43] Cf. also op. cit. Byström, Hans (2008).

- When designing structured MF products, especially MiCDOs comprising MFIs from different countries, the problem of FX risk arises. In the absence of hedging instruments like swaps, forwards, or options, the question is how to assemble a MiCDO to reduce the overall FX risk. To find a satisfactory solution, the question of pricing MiCDO tranches needs to be solved as well as the statistical modeling of the currencies used.

- Because every securitization and tranching of a portfolio of MFIs or MFs is unique, there is no general procedure for the valuation of structured MF products. Developing a set of tools especially designed for MF transactions remains a major challenge and would be extraordinarily useful.

- A further important long-term goal is to build local capital markets and financial institutions that are linked to the microfinance industry. One advantage of local capital markets would be, for example, the absence of currency risk. Furthermore, MFIs' fundraising in the local currency by local banks, including MFIs transformed into banks, leads to efficiency gains. If mainstream banks began to engage in microfinance, ordinary financial services would be available to the poor, who could therefore be considered as regular bank customers.

- The global financial crisis that began in 2008/2009 not only has an adverse impact on commercial banks, but also on MFIs. Especially the origination of MiCDOs has become practically unfeasible during the crisis, because investors have lost their confidence in structured products in the context of the financial crisis. The perceived risk of such investments is very high and investors therefore request high returns. The underlying assets do not generate yields high enough to pay the required returns. According to Tett[44] investors avoid structured products such as CDOs. Some practitioners even think MiCDOs will disappear completely as a result of the discredit of the whole financing method.[45] In keeping with Tett,[46] it will be difficult to regain the faith of investors in structured investments. Nonetheless, we think structured finance may be viable in some areas.

Since the future to this kind of refinancing instrument is unclear, we asked experts on microfinance capital markets about their views on the problems and chances of structured microfinance vehicles (SMFV). The results are presented in the following section.

---

[44] See Tett, Gillian (2009a): Bankers and bureaucrats seek a new philosophy. In: Financial Times, January 28, 2009, p. 4.

[45] See MicroCapital (2008): How far will the credit crunch affect the microfinance industry?, October 23, 2008, http://www.microcapital.org/microcapital-story-how-far-will-the-credit-crunch-affect-the-microfinance-industry.

[46] See Tett, Gillian (2009b): Lost through destructive creation. In: Financial Times, March 10, 2009, p. 9.

Results of a Market Survey on the Impact of the Financial Crisis 2008/2009 on Structured Microfinance

From April to July 2009, the authors conducted a web-based survey asking 132 MF investment experts on how they judge the market atmosphere of structured MF, in particular MiCDOs, with regard to the financial crisis. The addressees of the survey were affiliated to larger MFIs and institutions investing in or managing SMFVs. Furthermore, we asked a few academics. We used a standardized online questionnaire to facilitate anonymity. Responses from more than one person per institution were allowed. We collected 35 responses which represents a relatively high response rate of 26.5%.

Table 2 below provides descriptive statistics. In some of the questions, we ask for the level of agreement to presented theses. Thereby, the different levels of agreement follow a numeric rating scale as described in Table 2. In addition to the purely descriptive view, we apply the Wilcoxon signed rank test[47] to test for significance. Regarding the 35 responding microfinance experts as a representative sample, the test allows us to make conclusions on the whole microfinance investment scene. Whereas most questions asked the participants for agreement or disagreement with the theses presented, we test for both directions (agreement or disagreement) with a significance level of α=5% and the comparative neutral value corresponding to the null hypothesis.

The results of the analysis are presented and summarized below. First, the importance of MiCDOs is seen differently by the experts. The participants in our survey are sharply divided into two groups, one viewing MiCDOs as rather important, the other as unimportant. Second, the survey significantly confirms five of the possible advantages, namely improved access to capital markets by pooling smaller liabilities, reputation building, creation of different risk-profiles through the tranching process, diversification of funding resources and solution for the asymmetric information problem.

We cannot find any significant evidence suggesting that MiCDOs were seriously damaged by the financial crisis. The strong thesis that MiCDOs are even dead uttered by some bankers concerned with microfinance at the end of 2008[48] cannot be supported.

In the experts' opinion, the MiCDOs will recover fully within the next 3 years (starting in mid-2009). Nevertheless, there is evidence that they will not remain the preferred structured investment vehicle in microfinance. One possible alternative is (significantly) seen in structured MFIFs, like the EFSE, which also uses elements like tranches with different seniority.[49] The following refinancing in-

---

47 See Crawley, Michael (2007): The R book. Chichester: Wiley.

48 See op. cit. MicroCapital (2008).

49 See Ziller, D. (2007): The European Fund for Southeast Europe: An innovative instrument for political and economic stabilization, in Matthäus-Maier, I./von Pischke, J.D. (Eds.): Microfinance investment funds: Leveraging private capital for economic growth and poverty reduction. Berlin (a.o.): Springer, 193–212.

struments were also confirmed as important within the period 2010 to 2011: Deposits, donations, classical MFIFs, structured MFIFs, and private equity. MiCDOs and bond placement are not significantly regarded as an important refinancing source in that period.

We also asked the experts on how critically they see different aspects of CDO modeling in the context of the financial crisis. With the exception of dependency modeling, every aspect is significantly seen as critical, namely erroneous ratings of underlyings, the PD term structure modeling, the significance of tranche rating[50], and the complex structure. This result is a little surprising, since dependency modeling is in general seen as a very critical aspect of CDO rating and pricing, because it is often said to be one of the central aspects that led to a false estimation of the risk profiles of subprime credit CDOs.[51] However, there is significant confirmation of the dependency modeling issue on the 10% level.

Table 2. Summary of Microfinance Survey Results

	Question	Recoding	mean	median	sd	min	max	NA	N	sign.(?=5%)
1	How important is the role of CDOs in microfinance?	1=unimportant, 5=undetermined, 9=important	5.371	6	18.956	1	8	0	35	
2	Please rate the following advantages of CDOs in the context of microfinance!	1=I don't agree, 3=undetermined, 5=I completely agree								
2.1	Regulatory capital relief		3.0000	3	1.1282	1	5	1	34	
2.2	Solution for asymmetric information problem (e.g. originator keeps equity tranche)		3.3824	4	1.1014	1	5	1	34	agreement
2.3	Improved access to capital markets by pooling smaller liabilities		4.0294	4	0.9370	1	5	1	34	agreement
2.4	Reputation building for MFIs with recognized transaction partners		3.5000	4	1.1612	1	5	1	34	agreement
2.5	Improved access to capital markets by separating credit risk from inferior risk like country risk		3.1765	3	1.1407	1	5	1	34	
2.6	Creation of different risk-profiles through the tranching process		4.2647	4	0.9632	1	5	1	34	agreement

[50] This relates to the fact that risk profiles of CDO tranches have often been compared to those of equally rated bonds. By doing so, one ignores that CDO tranches react much more sensitively to systematic market changes than bonds. See Hamerle et al. (2008).

[51] See Choros, Barbara; Härdle Wolfgang; Okhrin, Ostap (2009): CDO pricing with multifactor and copulae models, Working Paper.

Table 2 (continued)

	Question	Recoding	mean	median	sd	min	max	NA	N	sign.(?=5%)
2.7	Diversification of funding resources		4.2059	4	0.9138	1	5	1	34	agreement
2.8	Fees		3.1515	3	0.9722	1	5	2	33	
3	How critically do you see the following aspects of CDO valuation in context of the subprime crisis?	1=not critical, 3=undetermined, 5=very critical								
3.1	Misspecified rating of under-lyings		4.065	4	0.9639	2	5	4	31	critical
3.2	Dependency structure mod-eling		3.29	3	0.9727	1	5	4	31	
3.3	Term structure modeling		3.419	4	0.7648	1	4	4	31	critical
3.4	Significance of a tranche's rating		3.71	4	0.9016	1	5	4	31	critical
3.5	Complex structure (e.g. CDO²)		4.032	4	10.796	1	5	4	31	critical
4	Is the image of MiCDOs seriously damaged by the current financial crisis?	1=I don't agree, 3=undetermined, 5=I completely agree	3.0000	3	1.0328	1	5	4	31	
5	We know that projects of launching new MiCDOs have been stopped. Are MiCDOs currently dead?	1=I don't agree, 3=undetermined, 5=I completely agree	2.7742	3	1.2572	1	5	4	31	
6	Do you think MiCDOs will recover again? When? Within ...	(not necessary)	2.2333	2	1.0400	1	5	5	30	within 3 years
7	Could investment funds with structured elements like tranching, waterfall structure ... be a sustainable alterna-tive to MiCDOs ...?	1=I don't agree, ... 3=undetermined, ... 5=I completely agree	4.0968	4	0.8309	2	5	4	31	agreement
8	How important will the fol-lowing instruments become to provide capital for Micro-finance Institutions (MFIs) within the next two years?	1=unimportant, ... 5=undetermined, ... 9=important								
8.1	MiCDOs		5.4516	6	2.2337	1	8	4	31	
8.2	bond-placement		5.6129	6	1.7640	3	9	4	31	
8.3	deposits		7.4516	7	1.2066	5	9	4	31	important
8.4	donors		6.9032	7	1.8139	3	9	4	31	important
8.5	classical MFIFs (Micro-finance Investment Funds)		7.3226	7	1.1941	5	9	4	31	important
8.6	structured MFIFs		6.7097	7	1.7549	2	9	4	31	important
8.7	private equity		6.3871	6	1.7258	3	9	4	31	important

Conclusion

MF may become an asset class. As the problems mentioned above are addressed, we may see more structured MF deals in the future, because structured MF is an investment instrument suitable for nearly all MF investors. A survey addressed to relevant world-wide experts on microfinance shows that structured instruments are regarded as an important means for refinancing microcredit lending despite the financial crisis. While experts disagree on how badly MiCDOs are affected by the financial crisis, they agree that MiCDOs should recover within a few years. As a first trace of evidence that the experts might be correct in their view that MiCDOs are expected to recover within a few years, four Indian MFI securitization deals were already observed in the year 2009.[52]

References

Ananth, Bindu (2005): Financing microfinance – the ICICI Bank partnership model. In: Small Enterprise Development 16(1), 57–65.

Bodie, Zvi; Kane, Alex; Marcus, Alan J. (2005): Investments, New York: McGraw-Hill.

Byström, Hans (2007): Structured microfinance. In: Journal of Structured Finance 13(2), 26–28. .

Byström, Hans (2008): The microfinance collateralized debt obligation: A modern Robin Hood. In: World Development 36(11), 2109–2126.

Compartamos (2010): Social, economic and human value: Strengths to keep on growing – annual report 2009, Banco Compartamos S.A., Mexico.

Choros, Barbara; Härdle Wolfgang; Okhrin, Ostap (2009): CDO pricing with multifactor and copulae models, Working Paper.

Crawley, Michael (2007): The R book. Chichester: Wiley.

Daley-Harris, Sam (2009): State of the microcredit summit campaign report 2009, Microcredit Summit Campaign, Washington D.C.

Dorfleitner, Gregor; Priberny, Christopher (2010): A quantitative model for structured microfinance, Working Paper, University of Regensburg.

Glaubitt, Klaus; Hagen, Hanns Martin; Feist, Johannes; Beck, Monika (2008): Reducing barriers to microfinance investments: The role of structured finance. In: Matthäus-Maier, I./von Pischke, J.D. (Eds.): New partnerships for innovation in microfinance, Berlin (a.o.): Springer, 249–378.

[52] See Matsukawa, Asako (2010). Is Indian microfinance the next subprime? In: Microfinance Insights 16.

Gonzalez, Adrian (2009): Microfinance at a glance – 2008, MicroFinance Information eXchance, Washington D.C.

Goodman, Patrick (2006): Microfinance investment funds: Objectives, players, potential. In: Matthäus-Maier, I./von Pischke, J.D. (Eds.): Microfinance investment funds: Leveraging private capital for economic growth and poverty reduction. Berlin (a.o.): Springer, 7–45.

Greer, Robert J. (1997): What is an asset class anyway? In: Journal of Portfolio Management 23(2), 86–91.

Hallahan, Terrence; Faff, Robert; McKenzie, Michael (2003): An exploratory investigation of the relation between risk tolerance scores and demographic characteristics. In: Journal of Multinational Financial Management 13(4–5), 483–502.

Hamerle, Alfred; Jobst, Rainer; Schropp, Hans-Jochen (2008): CDO versus corporate bond ratings: Comparing apples and oranges?, Working Paper.

Hartig, Peter (2011): The Role of Public and Private Investors for Structured Finance in Emerging Markets, in this volume.

Hüttenrauch, Harald; Schneider, Claudia (2008): Securitisation: A funding alternative for microfinance institutions. In: Matthäus-Maier, I./von Pischke, J.D. (Eds.): New partnerships for innovation in microfinance. Berlin (a.o.): Springer, 299–347.

Jansson, Tor (2003): Financing microfinance: Exploring the funding side of microfinance institutions, Inter-American Development Bank, Sustainable Development Department Technical Paper Series, Washington D.C.

Jobst, Andreas A. (2011): Structured Finance for Development – Outlook for New Applications, in this volume.

Koivulehto, Hanna K. (2007): Should we invest in microcredit? A financial analysis of microcredit from a USD-investor's perspective, September 2007, Vienna University of Economics and Business Administration, Working Paper.

Krauss, Nicolas; Walter, Ingo (2009): Can microfinance reduce portfolio volatility?, Economic Development and Cultural Change 58(1) (1 October 2009).

Ledgerwood, Joanna; White, Victoria (2006): Transforming microfinance institutions: Providing full financial services to the poor, Washington D.C.: World Bank.

Lopez, Cecar (2005): Microfinance approaches the bond market – the cases of Mibanco and Compartamos. In: Small Enterprise Development 16(1), 50–56.

Matsukawa, Asako (2010). Is Indian microfinance the next subprime? In: Microfinance Insights 16.

Maurer, Klaus (2011): Mobilising capital for the poor – How does structured finance fit in Emerging Markets? in this volume.

MicroCapital (2008): How far will the credit crunch affect the microfinance industry?, October 23, 2008: http://www.microcapital.org/microcapital-story-how-far-will-the-credit-crunch-affect-the-microfinance-industry.

Reddy, Rekha; Rhyne, Elisabeth (2006): Who will buy our paper: Microfinance cracking the capital markets? The realities of linking microfinance to local and international markets, InSight No. 18, Acción.

Rhyne, Elisabeth; Guimon, Andres (2007): The Banco Compartamos initial public offering, InSight No. 23, Acción.

de Sousa-Shields, Marc (2006): Commercial investment in microfinance: A class by itself? In: Matthäus-Maier, I./von Pischke, J.D. (Eds.): Microfinance investment funds: Leveraging private capital for economic growth and poverty reduction. Berlin (a.o.): Springer, 81–93.

Swanson, Brad (2007): The role of international capital markets in microfinance, Working Paper, Research Symposium "Credit Markets for the Poor", Columbia Business School, New York.

Tett, Gillian (2009a): Bankers and bureaucrats seek a new philosophy. In: Financial Times, January 28, 2009: p. 4.

Tett, Gillian (2009b): Lost through destructive creation. In: Financial Times, March 10, 2009: p. 9.

Yunus, Muhammad (2007): Remarks by Muhammad Yunus. In: Microcredit Summit E-News Bulletin 5(1), http://www.microcreditsummit.org/enews/index.html.

Ziller, D. (2007): The European Fund for Southeast Europe: An innovative instrument for political and economic stabilization, in Matthäus-Maier, I./von Pischke, J.D. (Eds.): Microfinance investment funds: Leveraging private capital for economic growth and poverty reduction. Berlin (a.o.): Springer, 193–212.

Index

L

M

N

O

P

R

MIX
Papier aus verantwortungsvollen Quellen
Paper from responsible sources
FSC® C105338

If you have any concerns about our products,
you can contact us on
ProductSafety@springernature.com

In case Publisher is established outside the EU,
the EU authorized representative is:
Springer Nature Customer Service Center GmbH
Europaplatz 3, 69115 Heidelberg, Germany

Printed by Libri Plureos GmbH
in Hamburg, Germany